D0404747

At The Heart Of The Matter

Copyright © 2004 Anne R. Bewley, Ph.D
All rights reserved.
ISBN: 1-59457-841-9
Library of Congress Control No.: 2004112612

To order additional copies, please contact us.
BookSurge, LLC
www.booksurge.com
1-866-308-6235
orders@booksurge.com

ANNE R. BEWLEY, Ph.D.

AT THE HEART OF THE MATTER

COMMUNICATING CARE IN HELPING RELATIONSHIPS

Harpwell Books
2004

At The Heart Of The Matter

TABLE OF CONTENTS

To All The Students Who Have Taken Psy 208,
Human Interaction In Helping Relationships, At Colby-Sawyer
College, New London, NH. As You Learned This Material,
You Taught Me How To Teach It.

INTRODUCTION

I know my job is to provide music for healing. But what if they want to talk? Am I just supposed to say 'uh huh, and what music would you like today?' Or is there some other way I can respond? It seems like when there is something big on their minds, the music doesn't flow right.

-- Marta, Certified Music Practitioner

Many times, when I am doing energy work, a client will start crying. I'm never sure what to do when that happens. I know listening is beneficial, but at times like that, just listening doesn't seem like enough. There must be more I can do to be helpful.

-- Joachim, Massage Therapist

I'm fine when it comes to the physical care of patients, but there are times when I think what the patient needs is just someone to talk to. I wish I knew how to help them.

-- Sully, Nurses' Aide

In my calling as a lay minister, I visit people who are shut in. So often they want to talk about their worries, but sometimes they get in too deep and I'm out of my league because I'm not a counselor. I don't know how to help and stay within my limits.

-- Betty, Lay Minister

I enjoy my work as a volunteer at the nursing home. I am comfortable when it comes to doing activities with the residents, but I wish I knew more about how to talk to them when there is something on their mind. I think if I did, I'd be a lot more helpful.

-- Leslie, College Student

Marta, Joachim, Sully, Betty, and Leslie are compassionate caregivers. They are well trained in their respective roles as helpers, but sense a gap in their repertoire of helping skills. Without tools for communicating in helping relationships and an understanding of the dynamics of helping interaction, they miss opportunities to be even more effective as helpers. This book is for them and for those like them—people whose primary job is not counseling, but who need solid knowledge and appropriate helping interaction skills to help them optimize their work.

At The Heart of the Matter emerged from my study in the International Harp Therapy Program. I entered the program as a harpist and licensed clinical mental health counselor. My goal was to make the transition from doing "talk therapy" to using music to heal.

Providing harp music at patients' bedsides and in other settings is the primary task of Certified Therapeutic Harp Practitioners. However, in my internship, I found that I drew on the verbal interaction skills I had learned when studying to be a psychotherapist to complement the use of the harp as an instrument for healing. Through the course of the International Harp Therapy Program, I noticed that some of my peers had good communication skills either because they came by them naturally or they had prior training or experience in helping interaction. Others expressed difficulty and discomfort engaging in a helpful dialog with the people with whom they were working. They were skilled musicians and keenly intuitive when it came to providing just the right music, but they were at a loss for words when interacting verbally. Here is an experience one therapeutic harp intern shared with me:

The woman was in tears when I came into the room with my harp. I asked her what was the matter, and she told me her tests had come back positive. She had cancer. I didn't know what to do. Even though I was there to provide healing music, it just didn't feel right to start playing. I needed to say something, but I was at a loss for words other than "I'm sorry." That sounded kind of lame to me, so I sat there. And that didn't feel right, either.

Therapeutic Harp Practitioners are *helpers* as well as healers and harpists. We engage with the people with whom we work, express an active interest in them, empower them to take part in the process of healing, and cultivate a relationship in which music can help. Although the focus of our work is therapeutic music, talking with the people with whom we are working is often a necessary part of our helping interaction. Taking advantage of opportunities to establish a relationship with them tends to make them more receptive to our participation in their care and to the therapeutic effects of the music.

From my vantage point as an experienced psychotherapist and educator, it seemed natural to write a book that addresses the need for a guide to interpersonal communication skills for helpers who are not trained as counselors. *At The Heart of the Matter* began as a resource for therapeutic harp practitioners. I was encouraged to include other therapeutic music practitioners, and then to expand to address the needs of other complementary caregivers.

When I told a friend what I was doing she jumped on the idea of developing her communication skills to help her manage her encounters with her students' parents. The volunteer coordinator at my internship site mentioned how useful this would be in training new volunteers. My intended audience kept broadening as I realized how applicable this information is to anyone who works with people in a helping capacity.

At The Heart of the Matter is as a primer, a source of information about effective verbal interaction, and a guide to learning when, how, and why to engage in helping dialog. The information and skills included are directed mainly to those who are learning helping interaction skills to augment their primary work with others. My examples are influenced by my practice as a certified therapeutic harp practitioner in hospitals and hospices, but the skills and ideas the examples illustrate are relevant in most helping situations. To provide a simple, clear, and easy-to-use resource, I condensed a complex process into a handbook, avoided using psychological jargon, and elected not to include research data.

At The Heart of the Matter will prepare helpers to interact beneficially and responsibly with the people they are helping. *It does not qualify readers to undertake the work of counselors or psychotherapists.* To be ethical practitioners, helpers who are not trained as professional counselors must keep clearly in mind the limits of their role and competence and obtain further education and credentials necessary to be qualified to do the work of counseling.

The core premise of *At The Heart of the Matter* is that talking about one's circumstances and events, expressing feelings, articulating beliefs, and telling stories to someone who is truly listening is healing, and that "healing moments" can occur whenever two people are engaged in an interpersonal encounter of any kind. These moments often present themselves when "talk therapy" is not the primary focus of the work at hand.

In a hospital setting, for example, patients may sometimes share their concerns with housekeeping staff who are in their rooms for reasons other than direct patient care. A simple "how are you today?" from a professor can prompt a sensitive disclosure by a student. Healing moments may be very brief, perhaps only three or four verbal exchanges, or they may constitute an extended conversation. Although these interactions may appear tangential to what we are there to do, they are opportunities to enhance and complement our work with those we are helping.

Taking advantage of healing moments requires the ability to recognize them when they occur, to establish and maintain an empathic connection, to listen and bear witness to what the other person says, and to respond in helpful ways. *At The Heart of the Matter* presents fundamental information and related skills in a way that facilitates understanding and application of knowledge.

In the first chapter, I define the nature of helping interaction, differentiate it from friendship and therapy, and explore the qualities of a healthy helping relationship and effective helpers. The next five chapters form the core of the book in which I discuss the fundamental skills of helping interaction—centering, listening, reflecting, responding, and asking questions. In the final chapters, I address several key issues that helpers must consider to remain ethical and effective practitioners and bring our exploration of communicating care in helping relationships to a close.

I made three editorial choices writing *At The Heart of the Matter*. The first was deciding what term to use to identify the people with whom we work. Client? Patient? Consumer? Parishioner? Student? Supervisee? Since *At The Heart of the Matter* is intended to be a resource for many kinds of helpers, none of these terms seemed suitable. Furthermore, all of these terms serve to identify people by their role, rather than their personhood.

As a mental health counselor, I have heard too many of my colleagues referring to the people with whom they work by their diagnosis: "You know that borderline we had in the other day?" "I wish I knew how to better work with our schizophrenic." People may have a diagnosable mental illness, but their illness should not define them. They are people. Joe is a "person with schizophrenia," not "a schizophrenic." Maura is a "person with borderline personality disorder," not "that borderline."

The same is true for those we help. They are people in a helping relationship with us. If we work in a hospital, they are people who are there as patients. If we work in a clinic, they are people who are there as clients. If we work in ministry, they are people who are there as members of the congregation. We must remember we are working with people, not the parts they play in a helping relationships.

My concern that no label seemed inclusive enough and that labels limit people to some feature used to define them, I elected to refer to the people with whom we work as "the people (person) with whom we work" and "the other person." I don't particularly like the word "other," because it highlights our separateness rather than our relationship, but in talking about two people in a relationship, I faced the need to distinguish one from the other. This gets a bit awkward at times, but perhaps those awkward points will remind us as caregivers that we are working with people, not a category.

At the same time I go to some lengths to avoid labeling the people with whom we work by the role they play. I contradict myself by calling those who work with those people (in other words, us) "caregivers" and "helpers" thus labeling us by our role. This way, I avoid a considerably awkward problem incurred by talking about "people who work with others" and the "people with whom we work." I also want to emphasize "giving care" and "helping," processes that are active in the relationships we have with those with whom we work. We help in many capacities—as ministers, teachers, helpers, volunteers, case managers, etc. Our roles are different, but our work is common in that we all engage with others in a helping endeavor.

The second editorial decision was the matter of gender. To avoid confusion, I refer to those of us in the role of giving care as "she" and the person with whom we work "he." I realize this evokes stereotypes, but I saw no other way to be clear about who was who in the helping relationship I describe.

The final editorial decision concerned writing style. Because *At The Heart of the Matter is* a book about interpersonal skills, I elected to write in a conversational style to "you," the reader. And because I, too, am involved in improving my skills with each interaction, I include myself, thus addressing "us," and I provide examples based on my own experiences. The other examples I use to illustrate helping skills are based on my experiences as a helper. These are intended to resemble "real life," but no particular individual.

I drew the material in *At The Heart of the Matter* from my years of education, training, and practice as a licensed clinical mental health counselor, and from my experience as a college professor teaching the theory and skills of human interaction in helping relationships. I have included the material I believe is most important in initiating and maintaining a healthy and beneficial healing and helping relationship.

Many theorists have influenced my thinking. I stand in the humanistic tradition, a psychological perspective that focuses on the essential experience of being human and the unique qualities of every individual as he progresses through life challenges and changes. Humanistic psychologists focus on health and wholeness more than on illness and dysfunction and more on the present than on the past. The ideas in *At The Heart of the Matter* are an amalgam of what I have learned from my teachers and so synthesized at this point in my career that I cannot distinguish clearly between others' ideas and my own variations on their ideas.

I have many people to thank for their inspiration and encouragement. At the top of the list is Christina Tourin, Director of the International

Harp Therapy Program. She is followed closely by those who have served as my sounding board, cheering squad, and editorial team, Page Rozelle, Ph.D., Jane Conklin, Margaret Bell, and Judith Coleman, M.A., L.C.M.H.C. I also thank Alice Kinsler, M.A., A.T.R., Manager, Therapeutic Activities Services at Concord Hospital, Concord, NH, for supervising and supporting my IHTP internship and for helping me integrate what I know about helping communication with my practice as a therapeutic harp practitioner at patients' bedsides.

CHAPTER 1
The Helping Context

Helping occurs within a relationship in which one person seeks assistance from another to meet a need, solve a problem, or reach a goal. Helping professionals have diverse backgrounds and training, and work in many different fields. All of them have one thing in common: the relationships in which the helper and the other person come together.

This chapter focuses on the helping relationship. We'll begin with a look at what a helping relationship is and explore three essential qualities of helping interaction. We will end the chapter with some thoughts to consider about what it means to heal and why relationships help us heal.

The Value of Helping Relationships

In the field of psychology, there has long been a debate about which approach to psychotherapy works the best. Interestingly, the research done to find the answer points to the fact that the most important factor in determining the effectiveness of any psychotherapy is the quality of the relationship between the therapist and the client, not the type of therapeutic approach the therapist uses. If the helping relationship is good, healing happens. If the helping relationship is not good, healing doesn't happen, and the potential for harmful effects increases.

Even though we are not helping others as psychotherapists, we are helping in a relationship with another person. We know that our particular way of helping (teaching, massage, therapeutic music, nursing, etc.) is important to the other person's wellbeing. Because our work together happens in a relationship, we need to take to heart the results of the studies on effectiveness of psychotherapy—that the relationship is the key to the success of the helping endeavor. Since the helping relationship is the healing force, our job as helpers is to create and sustain a special kind of interpersonal connection with the people we are helping. When that happens, our other work will be more successful.

Our relationships with those receiving our help will come in different forms. They may be one-time-only brief encounters, perhaps involving only an exchange or two between the other person and the helper. In a hospital setting, for example, a housekeeper greeting a patient as she enters the room saying "How are you today?" can receive a personal comment in return—"I'm sad because my daughter called to say she won't be in." A friendly greeting from a caseworker visiting a family at home can prompt a family member to burst into tears.

When we are attending a person going through long-term treatment or someone we are seeing on a recurring basis, we have an opportunity to sustain the helping connection over time. For example, a Reiki practitioner may work with the same person throughout his chemotherapy regimen. A physical therapist in a rehabilitation center will help someone who has had a joint replacement over the course of several weeks.

Regardless of the length of a helping relationship, there will be "healing moments" when the person with whom we are working is particularly open to receiving help. These are opportunities for us to provide emotional support and care with a word, a sentence or two, or a brief conversation. Although healing moments may appear tangential to the therapeutic process or irrelevant to our primary work, they are opportunities to enhance the treatment experience. Even if our practice does not include intentionally engaging in conversation the people with whom we work, they will engage us. Their desire to talk is an indication of their need to express themselves and unload their feelings and of their willingness to trust you to hear them. As helpers, we have opportunities to accept—or not—a momentary job expansion or shift in our primary role to listen and respond in a supportive way. When we do, the other person is likely to be more able to accept and benefit from what we have to offer as helpers.

Heidi is a therapeutic harp practitioner who plays for patients in a coronary care unit. Before playing for Mr. Schwartz, she has a brief conversation with him about the value of therapeutic music. During this conversation, Mr. Schwartz tells her how afraid he is about his heart condition. Heidi is able to respond in a way that helps him relax and benefit from her therapeutic music.

Heidi takes advantage of a moment to establish a helping connection with Mr. Schwartz. She suspends her role as a bedside musician to engage with him; she listens to him talk about his fears and communicates her care. Mr. Schwartz benefits from both Heidi's willingness to relate to him and her music.

We cannot make healing moments happen. What we can do, however, is set up the conditions in which they are likely to occur, notice when they happen, and take advantage of them when they do. We create those conditions when we cultivate helping relationships and pay attention to the way we interact with others.

Helping Interaction

The purpose of a helping relationship is to enhance the wellbeing of the person being helped. To accomplish this, helping relationships are structured so that the focus remains on the other person, not the helper. As helpers, we are as much a part of the helping interaction as the person we are helping, but our attention is directed at meeting the needs of the other person, not our own.

The focus on the concerns of one person in a relationship makes a helping relationship different from friendship. Friendship is a two-way street. We expect to help our friends, and we expect them to help us in return. We care about them, commit to them, and invest in them and the relationship between us; they do the same for us. In fact, if friends don't "get as good as they give" on a relatively consistent basis, they tend to drift apart and let the friendship fade. Mutual support and reciprocal benefit are part of what friendship is all about.

A helping relationship, on the other hand, is a one-way street and not intended to be mutual or reciprocal. We help someone else without an expectation that he will help us in return; we give, and the other person receives. Although we helpers benefit from our helping interaction with someone, the gifts we receive from helping should come from the process of helping, not from the other person. They are a satisfying side effect of working with others. The experience of relatedness that occurs when we are genuinely engaged with another person is important to our sense of belonging, as well as to our self-esteem and self-respect. It feels good to help others, but our feeling good is not the purpose of being a helper. Care of the other person is. Both people benefit, but the ways in which they benefit are not the same.

As a kind of helping relationship, the relationship between a psychotherapist or counselor and her client is also a one-way street. A good therapist invests in the therapeutic process, but she does not cultivate or depend on an attachment to the client. A client enters psychotherapy for his own good, not for the well being of the therapist. He may depend on and be attached to the therapist, but the spotlight is on him, not the therapist.

Good therapists know what their own issues are. They establish clear boundaries between themselves and their clients. A boundary serves as a psychological line between therapist and client so each can tell where the thoughts, feelings, and experiences of one end and those of the other person begin. Clear boundaries help therapists keep their own concerns on their side of the line so that they are out of the way of the client's work. Boundaries also help therapists avoid taking on a clients' feelings and concerns as their own. Many of the ethical decisions therapists make are based on the interpersonal boundary between them so that the helping relationship continues to be focused on the client and his wellbeing.

Although counseling relationships are helping relationships, they differ from the kinds of helping relationships we have with the people with whom we work in important ways. This difference is *depth*. Psychotherapists and counselors are there to help a person explore his thoughts, feelings, and concerns and find solutions to his problems. In our helping relationships the person we are helping may express deep feelings and talk about his problems or concerns. We can listen and respond in a way that reflects our care, but our scope of practice as helpers who are not trained counselors does not extend to diving into the other person's issues. Unless we have received formal education and earned professional credentials in counseling or psychotherapy, venturing into the deep places is beyond the limits of our competence, ability, and scope of practice. Doing so is unethical, and in most states it is illegal.

As helpers, we need to be friendly and remember that our purpose is not to be friends. We need to listen to and receive the other person's private thoughts and remember that our purpose is not to be a counselor. In healthy and effective helping relationships, we engage with others for the purpose of providing emotional support and facilitating the rest of our work together without the expectation of reciprocity in kind and with respect for our professional and personal limits.

Essential Qualities of Helping Relationships

Talking about our circumstances and telling our stories to someone who listens attentively and responds in a helping manner leads us to feeling valued and cared for. When we are heard, understood, and accepted, we allow ourselves to be more vulnerable and to open our minds and hearts to what the other person has to offer. Likewise, the people with whom we are working are more receptive when they know we care about who they are when we are working with them. We must build a relationship that communicates care and cultivates their trust for this to happen.

Psychologist Carl Rogers, one of the founders of humanistic psychology, described three qualities that are essential for creating and sustaining a helping relationship: empathy, genuineness, and positive regard. Rogers called them "necessary and sufficient conditions" for helping. They are necessary in that without them, the helping relationship will not develop and our efforts to help will be ineffectual. They are sufficient in that they alone are enough to establish the kind of relationship in which helping can occur.

Empathy

Empathy is a way of being, an attitude that we communicate to others by what we say and do. When we are empathic, we move toward understanding what the other person is feeling by using our heads and hearts to hear what he is saying.

Empathy begins with quieting ourselves so that we can listen and hear the other person's words, feelings, and inner messages. We step into his experience, sensing his world and viewing things from his perspective. Empathy is not, however, immersion in his experience. Even though we may identify with his concerns and circumstances, we must not get lost in them. When we are empathic, we shift between the other person's reality and our own, remembering that what is happening to him is not happening to us, and maintaining an internal boundary between us. We want to think and feel *as if* we were the other person, while knowing we are not—without losing sight of the *as if.*

The quality of *as if* makes empathy different from pity and sympathy. Pity means feeling sorry for someone else. We lose the *as* in the *as if* of empathy. When we pity someone, we do not move toward understanding what the other person is experiencing by stepping into his shoes. Instead, we stay detached and avoid his shoes altogether as we consider objectively or hypothetically how we might feel *if* we were in our own shoes in that situation. Our focus is not on how the other person is feeling, but how we might feel *if* we were in his position. We engage the other person with our heads, rather than our hearts, and the lack of the "feeling factor" makes us dispassionate—uncaring.

Sympathy, on the other hand, goes too far in the opposite direction. When we sympathize with someone, we take on his or her feelings and problems, making them our own. We lose awareness of ourselves and are no longer able to separate ourselves from the situation. Rather than maintaining the boundary between us and the other person, we become enmeshed in his experience and forget the *if* in the *as if.* We are there, fully immersed in the experience *as* it happens. We are wearing his shoes. Because we are experiencing what is occurring subjectively, we cannot understand the situation as an objective witness. When we are sympathetic, we come to the other person from our hearts, rather than our heads, and the lack of the "thinking factor" makes us passionate in the true sense of the word. We care too much, and we lose the perspective we need to be helpful.

Unlike either pity or sympathy, empathy is a matter of both heart and head. We use our hearts to encounter what the other person is experiencing *as if* it were happening to us, and we use our heads to remember that this is his experience, not ours. We step into the shoes of the other person, and we step back into our own. We identify with his experience, and we return to our perspective as helper. We are compassionate.

Genuineness

Genuineness is the second quality Rogers named as an essential component of helping relationships. People who are genuine come across as honest and open because they know how they are feeling and what they are thinking. It has been said that when people who are genuine smile, they smile with their eyes, not just their lips. People who are not genuine come across as phony. Something doesn't ring true about them They are not present as who they really are; they seem to be hiding behind an image or putting on a mask or pretending to be something they are not.

Gretchen is a nurse practitioner, and she's angry with Brent, a patient who has not followed the diet needed to help manage his diabetes. Brent's blood sugar readings are very high, and Gretchen has tried everything she can to convince him that he needs to take action, but nothing seems to work. She cares about his health, and she is concerned that there will be serious consequences as a result of his decisions about diet.

Gretchen suppresses her feeling because she considers herself a good nurse practitioner and believes that good nurse practitioners do not get angry with their patients. She smiles and tries to be calm as she tells him once again how important his diet is. But her voice has an exasperated tone that she cannot suppress, and Brent picks up on a mixed message. In spite of Gretchen's attempts to be cheerful and pleasant, Brent senses something underneath her words.

Genuineness starts with our being aware of an experience in the moment. Gretchen is angry, but she keeps that feeling out of her awareness. As a result, she is not being genuine. Genuineness would mean she acknowledged—at least to herself—that she is angry.

At times genuineness calls on us to disclose what is going on with us rather than keeping it to ourselves because doing so is what will enable us to be genuinely present in the relationship. However, we are mistaken if we think that genuineness means always revealing everything we think or feel, especially the way we are experiencing our thoughts and feelings. In fact being genuine often means *not* sharing all our thoughts and feelings with others because doing so would be contrary to our helping intent.

For example, it would not be helpful for Gretchen to react angrily to Brent or to threaten him with the dire consequences of his failing to do what he needs to do to live with his chronic condition. Instead, Gretchen could recognize her inner experience—anger, worry, and concern—and admit to Brent that she does feel upset about his lack of compliance because she cares about his health. Her inner and outer experiences would be congruent—what she is feeling and what she is communicating to Brent would match.

Positive Regard

Many of us grew up with what Rogers called "conditions of worth." We didn't feel worthy of someone's love unless we met some standard of lovability. We were expected to share our toys even when we didn't want to. We were only good enough if we got As. We were scolded if we said we wanted them to take the new baby back to where it came from—even if we asked nicely and said "please." We were hurt emotionally or physically when we expressed our feelings. Because love was (and is) important to us, we put aside the ambitions and feelings that didn't measure up to what others wanted for and from us, and we did what we needed to do to get the love we could, even though we might have wounded our sense of self in the process.

Relatedness is one of the deepest human needs. It should come as no surprise that finding ourselves in a relationship with someone who completely accepts us exactly as we are, without judging, measuring, and rejecting the lumps and bumps of our personhood, is a profoundly healing experience. Rogers called this complete acceptance *positive regard*. He considered it the third necessary quality of a helping relationship.

Positive regard is not the same thing as approval. Positive regard comes from appreciation and acceptance of another person's value and uniqueness as a person. Approval comes from judgment. We witness or experience something and call it good or bad according to our value system. When we say someone has our approval, we usually mean he is thinking, feeling, or behaving in ways we think he should, so approval has two aspects that are unhelpful. First, we are operating on *our* value system, not the other person's, and second, we are making a judgment about him.

Sara is a visiting nurse. She is currently helping care for Peter who has been diagnosed with cancer. Sara thinks Peter should take advantage of every opportunity for treatment. He has young children to help raise, a partner to love, work to be done, and a life to live. His decision to forego chemotherapy is very difficult for Sara to accept because she considers it a form of suicide, an act she considers morally wrong. Sara thinks Peter is being very selfish and unfair to his loved ones. She struggles to suspend her own value judgments and to accept Peter's right to make his own decision.

Sara does not approve of Peter's decision because of her own values. The reality is that we, like Sara, *do* judge others according to what we think is right. One of the keys to practicing positive regard is to recognize when our values are getting in the way of our ability to accept the other person. Sara realizes her situation and is making the effort to separate her feelings about Peter from her feelings about the choice he is making.

Practicing positive regard doesn't require Sara to approve of Peter's decision; it simply asks her to accept him as a good and valuable person, regardless of what he decides to do. It may be within the scope of Sara's practice to provide information, present alternatives, even challenge his thinking, but having positive regard for him means appreciating his uniqueness, worth, and dignity as an individual.

Empathy, genuineness, and positive regard help us weave a relationship in which helping can occur. They build a "container" for healing in which the people with whom we are working can regain wholeness of mind, body, and spirit.

In Western culture, we commonly limit our understanding of healing to the physical body where healing means diagnosing, treating, and eliminating a disease state. Under this definition, healing equals curing: Someone with illness would only be healed if the illness disappeared following treatment. Stepping outside this definition lets us view healing in a bigger picture and understand it as a process of restoring wholeness, an inner experience of completeness, and peace of mind that is independent of one's physical state. Under this definition, healing can happen whether or not a cure is possible.

A person with a terminal illness can heal, even if treatment cannot cure him. He can come to terms with his circumstances, complete unfinished tasks, pay his last respects to others, and prepare to die with a sense of integrity. Cases like this show us that healing is not necessarily about curing; healing a matter of making whole.

When we bring empathy, genuineness and positive regard and this perspective on healing together, we have a potential for helping that exceeds what we are able to do in our primary work alone. By paying attention to the quality of relationships we have with those we are helping and our qualities as helpers, we expand the impact of our interaction with others beyond helping to include healing. We more than meet the purpose of the helping relationship—to enhance the wellbeing of the other person. We support his growth toward wholeness.

Fundamental Helping Skills

Many of us who are drawn to professions in which we are helping others are inclined naturally to practice empathy, genuineness, and positive regard. We cannot rely solely on natural ability. To be compassionate helpers, we need to develop and strengthen specific skills so that we can build healthy helping relationships and best communicate our care.

Centering, listening, reflecting, responding, and asking appropriate questions are the fundamental skills that facilitate healing in relationships. They are necessary for communicating empathy, genuineness, and positive regard and are essential if we want to initiate and sustain a helping relationship. These skills are the building blocks of caring. Using them, we establish the connection and build a foundation for everything else that supports healing.

Each of the next five chapters addresses one of these helping skills. The skills build on each other, so they are best taken in order. Practicing them may seem awkward at first, especially as you focus on them one at a time. As you apply them intentionally and mindfully over time, they will become part of the fabric of your way of being with others, increasing your capacity for healing and improving the quality of all your relationships.

CHAPTER 2
Centering

The first step in establishing a helping relationship is preparing to be with someone. We need to pause and clear the thoughts, feelings, and distractions that can get in the way of our being fully present with another person. This process is called *centering*.

Taking the time to center before working with someone may seem impossible in a busy life. Who has the time when confronted with so many more urgent things to do? Centering may not be urgent, but it contributes greatly to our health and our effectiveness as helpers. Unfortunately for them and for those they help, many caregivers do not take the time to center themselves when working with others. They consider centering silly, tangential to their work, or otherwise unimportant.

When we are not centered, however, we tend to be distracted, make mistakes, "sweat the small stuff," compromise the quality of our interactions with our co-workers, and reduce our capacity to help others. Unless we are mindful and present, we really can't do anything else effectively. When we are centered, we are able to pay attention to others and respond in ways that build a good helping relationship.

This chapter provides an overview of several methods of centering, both as a daily discipline and as an "on the spot" tool in your work as a helper. Finding a centering practice that works for you will help you tune in to yourself and attune with others. You will be able to approach those with whom you are working ready to meet the moment mindfully and wholeheartedly.

ANNE R. BEWLEY, PH.D.

Using Silence to Center

Our lives are filled with noise of all kinds, welcome and unwelcome, harmonious and intrusive. Noise bombards us in the grocery store, at work, on city streets, and through the media. It distracts us from what we are doing, but we can become so accustomed to its presence that we don't realize that our focus is compromised. Engaging in conversation can be a noisy event, distracting us from true presence with others as we fill the space between them and us with chatter. It may be that only when we are silent do we experience the contrast between the distraction of noise and the attraction of stillness.

Our thoughts are a kind of inner noise that can interfere with our ability to be present because they insist that we pay attention to them. If we don't listen, our thoughts speak more and more loudly until we finally attend to them. Either we listen on our terms, when and how we want, or allow our thoughts to interrupt what we are doing and demand our time and energy. When we are silent, we notice what is happening in our mind and usually discover it is quite a busy place.

One of the main functions of the mind is thinking, so it makes sense that it should generate thoughts and ideas, form judgments, and identify needs. Like a monkey, it jumps from thought to thought without pause. This constant mental activity can interfere with our ability to experience our centered self. Staying aware of the present moment is a challenge because our attention naturally gravitates to our thoughts. By practicing silence, we learn to observe our thoughts without paying attention to them. We encounter our essential qualities and appreciate the experience of simply being still.

If you are drawn to the practice of silence as a tool for centering, I suggest you begin by finding a place and a time you can be by yourself without being disturbed. Since silence can be disconcerting at first, you may want to start your practice with one minute of silence and build up to twenty minutes or so as you feel more comfortable with the process.

Start by sitting in a comfortable position and take a few deep breaths. Focus your awareness on the experience of being still. You will notice sounds around you. Let them pass by like a breeze through a screen door. You can notice how busy your mind is. Be aware of your thoughts, but refrain from engaging in any thought. If you find yourself growing irritated or frustrated with the process, notice your feelings. If you find that you have followed a thought and drifted away from the moment, let it go and bring yourself back to your center. Sit in mindful awareness of all that is occurring and experience the gift of silence.

Silence can accompany an active or a receptive process. If you find it difficult to sit quietly, you can practice silence while you are doing something very simple, like taking a walk. Again, be aware of what is happening around you and inside of you. Notice it and let it pass through your attention rather than engaging with it. Feel what it is like to stay with every moment, every step, without being drawn away by noise, conversation, or thought.

Practicing silence teaches us to be present without having our concerns drawing us off center. Learning to be still and quiet makes silence a useful tool for centering before engaging in a helping relationship. We pause in a moment of silence in our office or in the hallway outside someone's room and allow inner and outer noise to come and go. We quiet ourselves with the intention of being with the other person without being in their way.

Using Breathing to Center

Paying attention to breathing causes us to focus on the present moment and ground ourselves in our bodies. Think about the times you have told someone (or someone has told you) to "take a few deep breaths" to help him calm down. It works.

Deep breathing helps us distance ourselves from whatever concern we have. When we are tired, frustrated, or caught up in worries, we sigh, expelling the air from deep within our lungs and freeing room for a big in-breath that helps us settle down, relax, and refocus. Taking a deep breath breaks up the pattern of distress and re-forms it in a way that leaves us feeling more ordered and centered. We can use this principle to help us order and center ourselves before meeting with others.

If you choose to use your breath as a means of centering yourself, start by becoming aware of and evaluating the way you breathe. Because breathing is an involuntary body process, most of us don't pay much attention to it. We simply breathe and go about our business. The problem is that we often do not breathe as well as we might, especially as we try to keep up the pace of daily life. Tension, stress, and other challenges get in the way of full, deep, relaxed breathing. Our breath becomes shallow, rapid, and limited to the upper areas of our lungs. As a result, we are only partly oxygenating our bodies, and we are causing more tension, more stress, and more challenges to our physical and emotional health.

As babies and young children we knew how to breathe properly. But somewhere along the line, as life got faster and more complex, we lost our natural rhythm and forced our breathing to conform to the world around us. Consequently, we can feel physically out of breath at times, especially when we are under stress. Whether or not we experience physical breathlessness as a result of shallow breathing, we may suffer from a kind of mental and emotional breathlessness. Just as in cases of hypoxia, the physical lack of oxygen, our psychological breathlessness can cause the thinking process to become muddled. We forget or overlook things. Our reasoning is unsound or incomplete. Our emotions bunch up out of lack of energy to cope with them. We lose touch with the stable place within, and compromise our ability to stand firmly in the present moment. Remembering how to breathe correctly remedies physical, mental, and emotional breathlessness and enables us to center ourselves in our bodies with clarity of mind and purpose.

Many meditation techniques employ "belly breathing," called diaphragmatic breathing because it engages the diaphragm, the expanse of muscle between the lungs and abdominal cavity. When we push the belly out, the diaphragm has space to move downward, causing air to fill the lungs. When we draw the belly in, the diaphragm moves upward, squeezing the air out of the lungs. At first, using the belly to help us breath can feel like we are breathing backwards because we are filling from the bottom up, rather than from the top down. Using the diaphragm to breathe enables us to fill the lungs entirely, getting air into the lower lobes rather than just the upper lobes. This better oxygenates the blood, reducing stress, inducing relaxation, and returning us to the present. Focusing on the experience of the breath moving through our nose and throat in and out of the lungs helps quiet the mind and focuses our attention on what is happening right now. If you would like to experiment with using breathing to center, find a quiet time and place to try this exercise:

Sit upright in a chair or lie on your back in a comfortable position and breathe as you normally would. Notice the feeling of the air moving past your nostrils and the back of your throat as you breathe in and out. Pay attention to where in your lungs your breath goes and how your chest rises and falls. Place the palms of your hands on your ribcage, allowing your middle fingers to touch just below your sternum and feel the movement beneath your hands as your lungs fill and empty.

After you have a sense of the movement of your chest as you breathe, begin your next in-breath by gently pushing your belly out and filling your lungs from the bottom up. This will expand your ribcage and cause your middle fingers to lose contact with one another. As you breathe out, draw your belly inward (up and toward your spine), pushing the air out of your lungs as fully as you can. Notice how your hands come closer together allowing your middle fingers to touch once again. Continue breathing slowly, using your belly, rather than your upper chest, to initiate the process of inhaling and exhaling. If you feel light headed, slow your breathing, taking time to pause at the still point between the in and out breath.

As you continue to breathe this way, check in with yourself. What differences do you notice in the quality of your awareness of yourself? Your alertness? Your sensations? Let your breath return to your usual pace and style, and notice any shifts you experience in the quality of your awareness and attention. When you open your eyes, take a minute to look around you. You may find that things look clearer, sharper, brighter, and more substantial than they did before. You also may feel calmer and more alert. What do you notice? (Note: After doing this exercise, stand up slowly to allow your body time to adjust to the changes in your breathing.)

Daily practice of belly breathing teaches us to breathe well. With regular practice, this way of breathing becomes more natural, and we can rely on it to help us center in our work as helpers. Try using belly breathing on the job: Before meeting the person with whom you are working, take a moment to stop and breathe in the same way you did in the exercise above. Feel your breath calming you, moving you out of the way and clearing an inner space for your encounter with the other person. After you have finished your work with the other person, check in with yourself. Notice how focusing on your breath before engaging with the other person influenced your ability to be present.

Taking a few good belly breaths with the intention of centering is a good way of preparing to meet any moment, in or out of a helping relationship. When a situation becomes difficult or we find that our emotions or thoughts have drawn us away from our center, taking some deep breaths helps us return. We pause and breathe out distraction and breathe in the sense of being centered.

Using Sound to Center

Sound has been used for tens of thousands of years as a way of creating community. It calls people together, enhances worship and ritual, heals, and alters consciousness. It goes directly to the deepest part of the brain where it affects our state of arousal, stimulates our pleasure centers, and influences our immune response; it can make us want to run, dance, weep, or relax. Therapeutic music practitioners know well the beneficial effects sound has on the bodies of the people they are helping. We can take advantage of these beneficial effects by using it as a tool for centering.

Sound can be used for the purpose of centering in two primary ways. One of them is through using our voice; the other is by using an instrument such as a bell or drum. Making vocal sound is a natural extension of the breathing process. Sound arises as breath passes through or past our vocal chords, tongue, teeth, lips, and nasal passages. We can make sounds that make sense (words), and we can make sounds that have no given meaning (tones).

One method for using words to help us center comes from a yoga practice of *mantra meditation*. A mantra is a word or short phrase that has special meaning to the user who chants or sings it aloud or repeats it silently to himself. When mantras are used regularly for focusing inward and centering, they take on a life and power of their own as a signal to the body and mind to calm, relax, and clear.

Some practitioners of mantra yoga receive their mantra from a teacher; others create their own. If you wish to try using a mantra for centering, you may want to find one that works well for you. Any word or short phrase that has meaning for you will work. Pick something that is not attached to a specific person or thought. For example, both the word "peace" and the name of a special friend can be meaningful, but "peace" will make a better mantra because it will not generate images, stories, and memories in the way that the name of a person or experience can. You will be linking your mantra to something new—relaxing and centering—and that's hard to do with a word that has old meaning.

It may be tempting to sort through and evaluate lots of words before settling on one. Since you can always change your mantra if you don't like it, allow yourself to pick one—or let it pick you. If you are still circling around in a whirl of words, try something like "one," "love," "God," or "health." I use "here" and "now," breathing in on one and out on the other. You could start by trying that if you want.

If you are drawn to experiencing mantra meditation, start by finding a time and place you can sit quietly for five or ten minutes.

Sit upright in a chair or lie on your back in a comfortable position and breathe as you normally would. Take a few deep belly breaths to clear your mind and signal your body to relax. As you begin to settle, start saying your mantra slowly and gently. Gradually decrease the volume of your voice to a whisper and then to silence as you shift from speaking to repeating your mantra to yourself. When you notice that your attention has wandered (and it will every few seconds), return to the sound of your mantra. Let go of any frustration due to your attention drifting. That is a natural process. All you need to do is notice that it has occurred and refocus on your mantra without self-criticism. When you feel ready to stop, let go of your mantra allowing it to fade into silence. Refocus your awareness on your breath, your body and the room around you, and open your eyes.

People who find mantra meditation helpful usually practice it on a daily basis for 20 to 40 minutes. You may wish to start with a shorter time and gradually increase it. Sitting in silence, making and listening to the sound of your mantra for just a few minutes every day can help you become more centered. In time, you may find yourself greeting life with more equanimity and engaging in all your daily activities more mindfully and wish to expand the time you give to mantra meditation.

Whether or not you practice mantra meditation as a daily discipline, you can use a mantra for centering in your work as a helper. Pause, take two or three deep breaths, and repeat your mantra to yourself a few times before meeting the person with whom you are working. You will find yourself more present and grounded in the helping relationship.

The power of a mantra comes from both the meaning of the word and the sound of the word, even when the "sound" is unspoken. We can capitalize further on the effect of the sound of mantras by a practice called *toning*, which is extending a vowel sound such as "ahh" or "eee". Tones differ from words in that they do not have meaning. Some people form multiple tones by using different vowel sounds separated by a consonant—"ah nee," for example. This is still toning as long as the consonants do not give meaning to the tone.

Toning works because of the effect of the vibration (frequency) of the tone on the body. Different sounds, volumes, and frequencies affect us differently, varying according to our individual physiological, emotional, mental, and energetic state. If you would like to experience the effects of toning, try the following exercise:

Find a time and place you can be alone. Sit in a chair with your feet flat on the floor, hands in your lap, and spine straight. Close your eyes and take a few deep breaths. On your next out breath, say the sound OOOO (as if "food"), sustaining it for a whole out-breath. Notice how this feels in your throat, mouth, head, and elsewhere in your body. Experiment with saying OOOO with your out breath, staying within your natural vocal range, but using different pitches each time. Notice how each pitch affects your body differently. Experiment with different volumes and notice what happens.

Now experiment with different vowel sounds: OH (as in "show"), AH

(as in "father"), AYE (as in "hay"), "EYE" (as in "high"), and EEE
(as is "need"). Try each of them on different pitches, too.
As you notice how different tones affect your body, find the sound,
pitch, and volume that resonates in your head. Feel the space inside
your head relaxing and clearing, and feel the flow of energy in your
head. Find the sound and pitch that resonate in your heart and feel
the relaxation and flow of energy there. Now find the sound and pitch
that resonate in your belly. Stay with that sound and pitch, saying/
singing it over and over with each extended out breath. Notice yourself
settling into your center and allow yourself to feel solidly present and
"at home" in your body in the moment. Pause to enjoy the experience
of being centered before letting the tone go and gently returning to your
present surroundings.

Toning is an excellent way of tuning in to yourself each day. There
may be times when you want to scan your body, "toning" each part into
harmony. If you find that your head, heart, or belly needs some attention,
you can tone to clear, soothe, and free it from distraction. Some people
use a range of pitches and vowel sounds to systematically clear, focus, and
center themselves on a daily basis. Others use tones as a tool for centering
in their helping practice.

Toning can provoke discomfort at first, mostly in the form of self-
consciousness. It can be very difficult for some people to allow themselves
to make meaningless sounds, even if they are by themselves. If this is
true for you and you still like the idea of using tones to center, you can
benefit from toning silently. Sit quietly and make the sounds without
making noise. Listen to them and feel the effects of them within yourself.
Learning to tone internally makes using toning as a tool for centering
more practicable for all of us when other people are around.

In addition to using vocal sound to center, we can use sound-making
instruments to help us. The acoustic vibration created by a bell or a drum,
for example, affects us physiological and psychologically. Our brains are
influenced by the physical properties of the sound waves, and our minds
are attracted to the sound itself. The mind has to let go of other activities
to pay attention to and follow the sound. The process of focusing on a
sound enables us to center in ourselves and in the moment.

If using external sound to center appeals to you, try experimenting with using an instrument.

> *If you have an instrument that rings—a bell, a chime, a bowl, or a gong—make a single sound with it. If you don't have a ringing instrument, strike the ends of a glass gently with a pen or pencil. Listen to the sound; let your mind follow it until it fades away. Repeat the process slowly for a few minutes, taking all the time you need to attend to the coming and going of each sound. Notice what happens to your mind and body. See if the process of attending to sound brings you into yourself in a more centered way.*
>
> *If you want to experience the centering effects of a drum, try beating on one softly and steadily in a "lub-dub" heartbeat rhythm. If you don't have a drum, you can beat on a hollow object such as a box or the bottom of a wastebasket or pot. You can also tap your hand on your thigh. Continue this for a few minutes, allowing your mind to focus on the sound and rhythm. Again, notice how your attention from the world around you shifts to the rhythm of the drum within you.*

Sound is a powerful dynamic. We have only begun to know its effects. Research indicates it has positive effects, calming us physically and soothing us emotionally. Both these factors contribute to our ability to be centered.

Using Imagination to Center

Sound works well as a tool for centering if you are an auditory kind of person. However, visually oriented people often prefer to use their inner eye to help center themselves. Using imagination this way means bringing to mind a picture of something that will serve as a symbol of centering. Like a mantra, this can be anything that holds meaning for you. Again, choose something that does not have specific meaning to you (your partner's face) or memories (the garden in your grandmother's garden), unless that meaning or memory will serve more as a symbol for centering than a stimulus for a walk down memory lane.

To use your imagination to center, begin by sitting or lying down in a comfortable position and close your eyes. Take a few deep breaths, allowing them to quiet your mind and relax your body. Pay attention to your thoughts without engaging in them, and notice how they can come into your mind as images, even though your physical eyes are not able to see. Become aware of what your mind sees.

As you sit quietly, imagine what "centered" looks like. What pictures does the concept bring to mind? A rooted tree? A circle? The center of a flower? A heart? A special place, real or imagined? Something else? Pick one of the images that particularly stands out—or let one of the images pick you. It may be tempting to sort through and evaluate a number of pictures before settling on one. You can always change your mind if a better one comes along later.

Focus on your chosen image, noticing the details in it. Move around it, explore it, and be present with it. As you do, remember that this is your image of "centered." Imagining it will call to mind your intention to center whenever you need to do so. After several minutes, let the picture fade from your imagination and gently return to your present surroundings.

Some people find it useful to bring their image into form. They find or make a picture or object, a talisman that represents their image, and carry it with them or post it where they can see it regularly. Having an object to hold also brings the sense of touch into the centering process. I have a small piece of blue glass that has a pewter Celtic knot embedded in it. I often carry this in my pocket as a touchstone. When I'm tense or nervous, I can put my hand in my pocket and feel its smoothness and remember to relax, breath, focus, and center.

Using Movement to Center

Some people find movement is an effective tool for centering because it brings them down to earth and into their bodies. Practitioners of yoga and other movement and energy practices know well how engagement of the body helps channel the body's energy and focus attention.

Within these practices, discrete postures and actions bring about and support an experience of being grounded. Although practicing them in isolation takes them out of their rich context, they can be adopted with respect as a tool for centering. A yoga teacher recommended a posture called "Mountain" as a way of clearing distractions and getting back into my centered self. She passed on the following instructions for experiencing Mountain. Try this posture if using movement to center appeals to you.

Stand with your feet about hip width apart and your arms hanging loosely and comfortably at your side. Feel your feet beneath you and get a good sense of being firmly planted on the ground. Breathing slowly and deeply, gently squeeze your buttocks, tucking your tail bone down. Lift up through your chest and sternum. Keep your chin down, and lengthen and straighten your spine. Lift your head up, as if you were trying to reach the sky.

Inhaling, raise your arms out to the side and above your head so that your palms are facing each other and your elbows are straight. Keeping your arms straight, lower your shoulders and lengthen your neck. Reach as high as you can. Continue to breathe deeply, feeling yourself strong as a mountain, grounded in the earth, stretching up into the sky. Breathe. When you are ready, turn your palms outward, slowly exhale, and lower your arms to your side. Breathe in and out and experience the sensations of having practiced Mountain.

If you want to use movement to center, you might choose to use Mountain at a specific time each day, such as when you get up in the morning. It also is something you could use in a private place in your work setting when stressful events throw you off center.

There may be cases in which using a whole-body yoga posture is not possible. We may not be physically capable of doing something like Mountain, or we may lack the space and privacy that best lets us experience the posture. In this case, we can do yoga with our hands.

Using the hands to communicate specific meaning is part of everyday life. For example, we shake hands upon meeting someone; we fold our hands in prayer; we wave a hand in greeting or farewell. *Mudras* are hand postures and gestures that come from the yogic tradition. They were developed with an understanding that there are energy centers and channels in the hands that we can access and direct for specific purposes such as centering.

Mudras are particularly useful as tools for centering because they need not be obvious to others and you need only the use of you hands to do them. For example, placing your hand over your heart for a brief moment may be a mudra that is centering for you and one you can do without straining your body or attracting unwelcome attention. Resting your hands palm up in your lap is an unobtrusive way of reminding yourself to center.

You can create your own mudra or experiment with ones that others have practiced for centuries. One that I use often in my work as a therapeutic harp practitioner is a traditional mudra that reminds me to approach the moment with love:

Sit or stand quietly with a straight spine, and place your hands in your lap. Take a few deep breaths. Hold your hands about six inches apart, gently rounded, facing palm to palm as if you were holding a ball. Curl your fingers slightly, and bring your hands together so your fingernails are touching. Stretch your thumbs away from your fingertips and bring the pads of your thumbs together. Notice how your fingers and thumbs form a heart. Take several deep breaths in this position before releasing the mudra.

Movement does not have to be complicated in order to be helpful. Walking and stretching are activities that clear the mind. Movement breaks up routine, gets blood flowing through the body, and helps muscles relax. Simple movement on a regular basis is an antidote to stress and guards against building up tension in the body. Yoga postures, mudras, and light physical activity are excellent ways to attend to the body and to center.

Using Scent to Center

The smell of incense or aromatic oil can serve as a tool for centering, especially when we allow ourselves to sit still and follow the fragrance as we breathe. Using incense or aromatic oils can accompany and augment the effects of the other centering exercises. The practice of aromatherapy attests to the healing effects of scent.

However, many people are extremely sensitive to odors, and because of this, increasing numbers of work centers are making the commitment to be "fragrance free." Helpers in these settings are asked to refrain from wearing perfume and other products that have a scent. Since we do not always know who is adversely affected by fragrance, we should avoid wearing scents in any setting in which we work, regardless of whether they are designated as fragrance-free. Using scents at home may be something you want to add to your centering practice, but do not use them at work.

Summary

Centering is the first thing we must do before we can help someone else. When we are not centered, we are not fully present. We tend to listen with half an ear and respond automatically, without really considering what the other person is saying. We may greet the person with whom we are working feeling (and looking) scattered and unfocused. Our movements may be abrupt and clumsy, or our tone of voice may be sharp and unwelcoming. Once we center, we can attune to the other person and respond in ways that are truly helpful.

If you do not already have a centering practice, I encourage you to try the methods described here. Find one that works for you and make it your own. Use it as a daily discipline, and apply it on the job. Over time, it will become part of your habit of being, your natural response to events that pull you off center, and a strong foundation for the rest of your helping interaction.

CHAPTER 3
LISTENING

Once we are centered and fully present, the primary task in the healing encounter is listening. We are there to hear what the other person has to say. In this chapter, we'll explore what listening is, identify obstacles to effective listening, and describe how to listen.

The Process of Listening

We usually think of listening as something that happens through our ears. Although listening involves hearing—one of the physiological functions of our ears—it also involves sight, sense, and intuition. In addition to processing the sound of someone's words, we can see what is said nonverbally by observing the other person's facial expressions, body postures, and movements. We may also find ourselves seeing images with our inner eyes—the imagination—that serve as illustrations or metaphors of what the other person is saying.

Listening also occurs through when we sense the energy behind another person's words. We literally feel (sense) what is being said, particularly picking up the unspoken emotions underlying a message. Finally, listening occurs through intuition, a process by which we know what another person is saying without a logical basis for that knowing.

To listen, we have to pay attention to what the other person is saying. Whether or not we hear and understand what he wants to tell us depends in large part on how well we attend to him as he is speaking.

Non-listening occurs when we are with another person but not paying attention to what he is saying. We are distracted by events within or around us. Our ears receive the sound, but our minds and other ways of hearing do not give meaning to what we hear. We may pretend to listen (we might even fool others into thinking we are listening), but we don't really hear what the other person is saying.

Partial listening is a process of filtering out everything but what is meaningful or relevant at the moment. When we practice partial listening, we pay a little bit of attention to what the other person is saying, letting most of it go and trapping what we want to hear. Our attention comes and goes, depending on what is being said. All partial listening is self-oriented in that we are not particularly interested in what the other person has to say except as it pertains to what we consider important in our own lives.

Effective listening occurs when we give full attention to the other person and express through eye contact, facial expression, body posture, and movement that we are sincerely interested in hearing what he has to say. We withdraw our attention from a focus on other activities and step outside our own concerns—particularly our reactions to what the other person is saying—to listen with all our senses.

Effective listening is an active, but relatively silent process. We receive and hold what a person says without comment or question about the message until after he has finished. Effective listening requires the readiness to be present, a desire to know and understand what is meaningful to this person at this time, and empathy and positive regard for the other person. We must want to listen, be interested in what the person has to say and willing to make the effort and take the time necessary to hear.

Obstacles to Effective Listening

Messages go through a rather complicated process as they go from sender to receiver, even when viewed apart from the complex processes of the brain that let us think, speak, and understand words in the first place.

AT THE HEART OF THE MATTER

Michael has an idea he would like to communicate to Gerri. First, he has to choose words to express his thoughts. He selects these from his "inner dictionary" of words and meanings, and he constructs his message according to the grammatical rules of the language he is using. He then uses his voice to say the words out loud.

Gerri's ears pick up the sound waves created by Michael's voice. She makes sense of what she has heard by assigning meaning to the sounds heard using her own "inner dictionary" of words and meaning. If Gerri has heard the words Michael has said and considers those words to have the same meaning Michael does, she probably understands what he has said—at least at the verbal level.

When he sends his message, Michael, like any communicator, automatically includes more than words in his message. He says them in a certain tone of voice, at a certain volume and speed. He gives his message added meaning by stressing some words more than others. He uses facial expressions, hand gestures, or other movements to make the message understood. An energetic quality to what he is saying communicates how he feels about what he is saying. To really understand Michael's message, Gerri must "hear" all these nonverbal cues and interpret them the same way as Michael.

This communication could go awry in many places, with the result that Gerri does not hear the same message Michael sent. Michael's words may not mean the same thing to Gerri as they do to him. His speech may have been unclear or inaudible. Gerri's sense of hearing may not be acute enough to pick up on all the sounds of Michael's words. The washing machine may have hit the spin cycle and drowned out the sound of Michael's voice just as he was getting to his point. Gerri might be preoccupied by thoughts and feelings about something else so that she is only partly listening to Michael.

Three categories of potential obstacles are in this list: physical deficiencies, internal noise, and external noise. If a problem exists with certain areas of the brain, the voice, or the physics of hearing, communication through speech may not be possible for both people. In that case, the helper and the other person must find other ways of exchanging messages. Exploring how to communicate with people who cannot speak is important, but outside the purview of this book. Helpers who work with people who are deaf or who have had strokes, are on mechanical ventilators, or are otherwise impaired in their ability to speak and process spoken messages should explore strategies for communicating in those situations.

Noise is one main obstacle to effective listening. In many settings, external noise is the culprit—the sound of others' voices, medical equipment, TV or radio. These sounds can distract us from what the other person is saying. They also can interfere with the physical aspect of hearing. The TV may be too loud, or the sound of the heart monitor or suction device may compromise our ability to hear what is being said. Another person's impaired speech also qualifies as external noise because it occurs outside of us and can interfere with hearing what he is saying.

Internal noise occurs when our minds engage in a process other than listening. We may be involved with other concerns in our lives, such as worry about a sick child, anticipation of an upcoming meeting, or thoughts about the last person we visited. We may short-circuit the listening process by thinking about how we are going to respond. For example, a person with whom we are working may be talking about upcoming surgery. We think we know the other person is going to tell us he is scared, so we complete the message in our minds before he says it. In our haste to formulate a reply, we can end up saying something that has little to do with the real point of the other person's message.

Inner noise also can be generated by the emotional and cognitive filters we have. Each of us has been conditioned by society, culture, subculture, and family to think in certain ways. We have a lifetime of unique experiences. We have ideas about the way things should be, our personal value system, and our biases and prejudices. We associate particular words, nonverbal behavior, and language cues with specific experiences so that they have a different meaning for us than they might for others. We have issues that can be triggered by a certain tone of voice or turn of phrase resulting in a rush of emotion.

Our mind processes all information—including the messages we receive from others—through these filters. As a result, what our mind thinks is the message is only the message as it has been vetted by our belief systems and experiences. A popular saying puts it this way: "I know you believe you understand what you think I said, but I'm not sure you realize that what you heard is not what I meant." Our filters can skew what we hear in such a way that we do not understand what the other person really means.

Eliminating or reducing external noise is easy. We simply need to notice it and do something, for example, close the door or ask permission to turn down the TV or radio. We may have to move closer to the other person and invite him to speak more slowly or to repeat what he has said. Managing inner noise is more of a challenge, however, because the noise is related to us—our own concerns, reactions, and points of view—and we usually find it harder to distance ourselves from it. We may be able to eliminate or mitigate outside noise, but we can't get rid of inside noise. Instead, we need to acknowledge it, decide to let the inner noise coexist without interfering with our desire to listen, and refocus our attention on the other person. The best way to do this is through centering, because centering gets us back to ourselves and the moment and helps mute the internal noise so that we can be fully present and ready to listen.

Listening to Non-Verbal Messages

Our ability to create and use language to express ourselves is part of what makes us human: much of our communication occurs through the use of words. When we listen, words are what we hear and the vehicle through which we convey our message. Along with our learned ability to communicate through language is our natural and culturally determined ability to communicate through body language and energetic and vocal accompaniments to verbal language.

Social psychologists have determined that some body language is universal. For example, people in all cultures smile to express positive emotion, frown to express displeasure, and grimace and stick out their tongues to express distaste or disgust. In most cultures, forming a fist communicates aggression and extending the arms underside up and palms open suggests friendship or invites embrace.

On the other hand, some body language is culturally specific. For example, the "A-OK" joining of the tips of the thumb and first finger means everything is in good condition and all set to go in North American culture. In Italy, the gesture is obscene. Resting one ankle on the opposite knee is a common and perfectly acceptable way of sitting in a chair in North America. In Asian countries, showing the sole of your foot someone is an insult. White North Americans tend to move their eyes while talking and look at the speaker when they are listening. Native Americans tend to do it the other way around, looking at the other person directly when they are talking and averting their eyes when they are listening.

Although some body language is universal, however, we must be careful not to assume we know what someone is saying through facial expression, body posture, or eye contact. What we see may contribute to what we hear, but because of the cultural and human ambiguity of body language, we should never take a hunch about non-verbal messages as truth. We should consider body language possible information, rather than fact.

Much of what we hear when someone speaks is sound other than words. "Please go away" can hold several different messages depending on how it is said. When someone says it sharply, we sense that he might be annoyed and that we would be better off doing as we are asked. If someone says the same thing in a whiny voice, we may suspect that they really want us to stay. "How are you feeling?" can sound patronizing if asked matter-of-factly, it can sound caring and concerned if spoken gently, slowly, and warmly. "Good for you!" may be encouraging, enthusiastic, and sincere, or sarcastic and mean-spirited, depending on the tone of voice.

The quality of pitch, tone, rate, volume, fluency, and pressure of speech are usually cues to emotions. We sense when someone is excited, angry, sad, or afraid from the way they are speaking. Remembering that the meaning of these aspects of speech, like body language, is not necessarily universal and may be due to factors other than the message is important to understanding communication. Pain, for example, will skew the picture, adding a tightness and tension to the voice that is not related to displeasure or anger. If we don't know that someone has just received a sedative, we can misconstrue his slow speech as sadness or depression.

Since non-verbal information is available to us and because much of what we communicate to others happens in non-verbal ways, we are wise to take into account all that we hear with our ears, eyes, and other senses when we are listening. But when we come to making sense of what we are hearing, we must remember the ways in which what we are hearing may not be what others want to us to understand.

Three Messages in One

The verbal and non-verbal messages we give and receive have at least three components: *content, emotion,* and *meaning.* Effective listening involves hearing these three levels of disclosure in the other person's message.

Content has to do with the subject or topic of the message: *"My daughter is having another baby." "The nurse just told me that my surgery has been delayed." "They told me I have to take off my necklace, and I don't want to."* If the other person is not confused or disoriented and does not have impaired speech, the content of the message is usually easy to identify.

Emotion has to do with the feelings related to the message content. If a person says, *"I'm really upset because the nurse just told me my surgery has been delayed,"* the feeling is explicit. He has told us he is upset. Another person may not tell us he is upset about this situation, but the emotion attached to his disclosure that his surgery has been delayed may be evident to us by an edge of anger or a frown that tells us he might be frustrated, angry, or worried. In this case, the feeling is implicit; we infer it from what we have "heard" with our other senses.

Meaning has to do with the importance of the concern to the other person and is usually related to his value system or experience, or to a deeper matter. Most of the time, meaning is not explicitly expressed. We might intuit it—though this can be dangerous unless we check out our hunch—or it might become evident as the other person says more. *"I'm scared that my test results are delayed,"* said someone with whom we are working. The reason this fact is important to him is because he believes that a delay means bad news. *"They told me I have to take off my necklace, and I don't want to."* For this person, the necklace represents healing, and taking it off would contradict the desire to heal.

When we listen to what someone has to say, we often limit our listening to the level of content. If the feeling is explicit, we may pick up on it. What we don't often hear is the meaning behind the message, the experience that is closest to the other person. Sometimes this is because we do not want to hear or know the meaning in a concern. That information may seem too intimate, or it may be too similar to something we are feeling or that is important to us.

It may be helpful to remember that at this point in the helping interaction, we are just listening. Our task is to pay attention and receive what the other person tells us, verbally and nonverbally. We do not need to say or do anything other than hear what the other person is saying.

Listening Action

Listening is largely a silent practice, so how do we communicate that we are present and hearing what the other person has to say? The answer to that lies in our own nonverbal signals. As we observe people's body cues for messages, they are reading our posture, position, and facial expressions to see whether we are listening. Our silent presence communicates a great deal, but it must be backed up by our actions if someone is to be convinced we are truly there.

Paying attention to two or more things at one time is impossible. We may think we can—we may even consider ourselves excellent multi-taskers—but what we are really doing is shifting our focus back and forth from one activity to another. Our attention to each task is intermittent. If we are preparing a meal *and* washing dishes *and* feeding the dog, we aren't really doing everything "all at once." Instead, we are moving quickly from one task to the next. Add to this activity a conversation with a partner, child, or friend. Can we listen empathically while continuing to do the other things you are doing? I think not. Effective listening requires full attention, and that means we need to choose to suspend other action. Either we listen, or we don't.

This lesson was brought home to me by my son:

I was in the kitchen frantically attending to a variety of chores when my son came in looking a little despondent. When I asked him how his day had gone, he began to talk about some problems he was having. I listened and made some suggestions, but I felt tense and frustrated because he didn't seem to be moving off his point.

I asked him what else was happening, and he muttered, "You haven't even heard what I just said." I was brought up short just as a defensive protest formed on my lips. Fortunately, I didn't say those words. Instead, I took a deep breath and centered myself. "You're right," I said, turning off the water and the stove. "Let's sit down so I can really listen to what's up." What followed was one of the best conversations we have ever had.

Because I know I cannot do two or more things well at the same time, I do not take notes in counseling sessions. First, if I'm taking notes, I'm not listening fully. Second, if I'm writing, I'm not showing the other person that I am interested in listening. If I must write for some reason, for example, if I'm taking a history on a form, I will tell him so and ask him to pause so I can get my ideas down on paper and then give him my full attention again. Since that conversation with my son, I've tried not to fool myself or anyone else into thinking I can listen fully and do something else at the same time.

The best physician I ever had was one who came and pulled up a chair and sat as he listened to what I had to say before asking any questions or saying anything himself. Because he wasn't doing anything else—flipping through my chart, fussing with his instruments, getting the examining table ready, cleaning his glasses, or seeming preoccupied with more important things—I felt like he really cared about and was interested in me as a *person*, not just a patient. He gave me his time, and he heard my concerns.

One of the first things we can do to show the people with whom we are working that we care and are interested is to pause to be with them when we first enter the room before doing anything else. If the other person wants to talk, we can listen without providing distraction. During our time together, when we are doing something else (playing the harp, adjusting his IVs, preparing for a massage or examination), we can stop what we are doing—or ask for a few seconds to finish up—before trying to pay attention. Our very *inaction* communicates our attention.

Considerable research has been done on the kinds of body posture and positions and other non-verbal actions that communicate listening in American culture. Again, we must consider subcultural differences, but for the most part, we communicate we are listening when we sit or stand quietly. We have an appropriately open body posture, our arms and legs are uncrossed or loosely crossed at the knee or ankle, and we are turned toward the other person at an oblique angle or seated slightly off to the side. In many cultures—including most North American cultures—facing someone squarely can communicate aggression. Adding close proximity to such a position can suggest physical intimacy. Neither is appropriate in a helping relationship.

When we listen we tend to respond naturally with our faces. Our eyes reflect the sorrow we hear, our smiles communicate appreciation. For the most part this is good. However, we should remember that our faces also can communicate disapproval and judgment and leave those expressions behind if we are going to communicate empathy as we listen.

Along with facial expression tend to come short verbalizations such as "Uh huh," "hmmm," and "I see," which tell others we are following what they have to say and encourage them to continue. They serve as catch up points in a conversation. When we hear one, we know someone has followed what we are saying up to that point. When they are not there, we wonder if the other person is.

Because we communicate both verbally and nonverbally at the same time, people send two messages at once. Mixed messages occur when verbal and nonverbal messages do not say the same thing. For example, a person with whom we are working may tell us he is "just fine" even when his face is etched with pain or he has a glum expression on his face. An elderly resident of a nursing home may tell us he is not concerned about his upcoming doctor's appointment while fidgeting and looking worried at the same time. We need to listen to both messages in cases like this, noting the contradiction to ourselves. When it comes time for us to respond, we may need to check our understanding of exactly what the message is. (We will discuss this further in the chapter on responding.)

Listening To Silence

One of the keys to effective listening is appreciating and respecting the silences that occur in conversations. When someone is ill, distressed, or not able to put his thoughts into words or speak clearly, listening through the silent moments, rather than filling the silence, gives the other person time to think about what he wants to say and to find the best way to say it. When a person is dealing with strong emotion and at a loss for words, being quiet helps us hear the emotional and other messages that reverberate in silence.

Silence can be difficult to experience. Until we are accustomed to it, silence can feel very uncomfortable, and we can feel compelled to fill it. Saying something may be the best course of action (more on this in the next chapters), but pausing and waiting out a brief silence is one of the best ways to encourage another person to talk about his concerns.

Summary

Listening is one of the greatest gifts we can give others. In the listening moment, we set aside our own concerns and suspend judgment to receive what is being said. We are present as another person shares himself with us in some small way, and we value what he offers. By hearing all that he says—verbal, non verbal, content, feeling, and meaning—we witness his experience, exercise empathy and positive regard, and communicate care.

CHAPTER 4
Reflecting

Listening, like centering, never really stops in a healing encounter. Effective helpers continue to listen to what a person is saying even when he has stopped talking. At some point, however, he will finish, and there will be an opportunity or a need for us to speak. What we say first and how we say it will greatly influence the other person's willingness to continue to express himself. Our initial reply to the disclosure can come in several forms, including reflection, response, and inquiry. These skills are related, but different. In this chapter, we will explore the purpose and process of reflection.

Purpose of Reflection

When we reflect what another person has disclosed, we act as a mirror, showing the other person the message we have received. Reflection communicates our attention in words and allows us to check the accuracy of our understanding. Once we have reflected a message, the other person is likely to do one of two things: correct or confirm us. If we miss the point or an important part of the message, he will restate his message and give us another chance to hear it. If our reflection indicates that we understand what he is saying, he will acknowledge it and stop because he has said what he has to say or continue. Reflection also acts like the "save" function on the computer. It backs up what the other person has said so that it isn't lost when something new is added. It provides focus, direction, structure, and emphasis in the healing exchange. The spotlight is on what the other person thinks and feels is important, and the conversation moves along the lines of the concerns.

Take a look at how these dynamics might play out in a healing encounter.

Helper (H): How is your day today, Mr. Jones?
Other Person (OP): Not so good.
H: It's a bad day. [The helper reflects what she thinks she heard.]
OP: It's not that, it's just that my leg hurts. [The other person corrects the helper and clarifies his message.]
H: Your leg is hurting. [The helper responds to the other person's correction with a more accurate reflection.]
OP: Yes. I can't relax. [The other person confirms the helper's understanding and adds more to what he has said.]
H: The pain keeps you from relaxing. [The helper reflects the other person's addition to his message.]
OP: Yes. [The other person is satisfied that the helper understands his message.]

In this exchange, the caregiver's initial response misses the mark. The other person corrects her, and the helper gets back on track with a reflection that focuses more directly on what is relevant. The other person adds to his message once he knows that the helper understands. The helper reflects the additional message. The other person confirms it, and both are satisfied that helper has heard and understood what is of immediate concern to the person being helped. At this point, they are ready to move on.

Reflection also serves as a magnifier or sounding board, making the other person's message bigger, clearer, and louder than it was when spoken. By distilling out and reflecting back what we see and hear, we enable someone to see and hear himself, better understand his own concerns, and feel more settled or able to take the next step. The following example illustrates this process and highlights how empowering being heard and understood can be for those with whom we are working:

OP: I'm not sure about this new doctor. I wish I had my old one back.

H: *You'd rather have your old doctor than the new one.* [The helper reflects.]

OP: *You bet. This new guy looks like a college kid.* [The other person continues, indicating he feels understood.]

H: *He seems pretty young to you.* [The helper reflects.]

OP *(with a worried look): Do you suppose he knows what he's doing? I don't want to be a guinea pig.* [The other person continues, indicating he feels understood.]

H: *You're worried about whether he has enough experience.* [The helper reflects the patient's nonverbal emotional message.]

OP: *I trusted my old doctor. I don't know this new guy.* [The other person refines his message and modifies the helper's reflection.]

H: *Your old doctor was someone you knew and trusted, and the new guy isn't.* [The helper reflects more accurately.]

OP: *This surgery is a big deal. I'm afraid that things won't come out all right. If I just knew how much experience this new doctor had with this procedure, I'd feel better.* [The other person continues, indicating he feels understood.]

H: *You'd feel more comfortable if you had a better idea of what this doctor's experience was.* [The helper reflects.]

OP: *Yup. Maybe I could ask him. Yeah, that's a good idea. I think I'll do that the next time he comes in. Thanks.* [The other person reaches his own conclusion.]

By continuing to reflect the other person's concerns, the helper has helped him move forward with his thinking. It might have taken less time for the helper to suggest he ask the doctor about his experience with the upcoming procedure once his concern became apparent. However, by listening and attending to the other person's messages and reflecting back the essential points, the helper enables him to come to this idea himself. The person being helped thanks the helper, but he is the one who has taken charge of his situation and found his own solution. The helper has done nothing but listen attentively and reflect back an understanding of what the other person has said.

Kinds of Reflection

In general, reflection is any response that mirrors the other person's message. The helper can match the other person's words exactly, she can restate the other person's message using slightly different words, or she can put the other person's message into her own words.

When we repeat all or part of what the other person has said using his words, we are reflecting in the form of *repetition*. This can be as simple a matter as repeating a single word:

> *OP: I'm psyched because I get to go home today.*
> *H: Psyched.*

Or it can be a replica of the whole statement with a change of pronoun from "I" to "you":

> *OP: I'm psyched because I get to go home today.*
> *H: You're psyched because you get to go home.*

Repetition is useful when a conversation is flowing well, and our intent is to keep up with the other person and encourage further disclosure. It also is very useful when ambiguity exists in the other person's message or we are unsure of what his point is. Through a word or two, we can show we are present and listening and leave room for the other person to elaborate. If we are unsure of what the other person means, we can indicate our desire for clarification or more information by lifting our voice at the end of the repetition as if we were asking a question:

> *OP: I don't like what's happening around here. It's all very confusing to me.*
> *H: You're feeling confused…*

The caregiver is not sure what the other person is confused about, but she picks up the message and reflects it back to the speaker and opens the door for the other person to say more about his confusion.

When we first use repetition as a tool for reflection, it can sound stilted, even silly. Repetition is a simple skill, but one that is very common and not as silly as it can sound. If you listen to your everyday interactions with others, you will realize how often you repeat what you hear as a way of showing you are paying attention and following the speaker. A casual conversation like this would not be unusual:

Person #1: I'm going shopping today.
Person #2: Shopping...
Person #1: Yeah, I need a new suit.
Person #2: A new suit...?
Person #1: My girlfriend asked me to this formal dance, and I don't have the right kind of clothes.
Person #2: You don't have the right clothes.

Of course, too much repetition can leave us sounding like we aren't paying attention, so as a skill reflection is most useful in small amounts. It must always be used with the sincerest intent. If what we are saying carries even a hint that we are mimicking or mocking the other person or repeating what he is saying without empathy and positive regard, repetition fails to be helpful.

Repetition is an exact reflection of all or some of another person's message. When we stay close to what the other person has said, but do not repeat it exactly, we are reflecting in the form of *restatement.* Using restatement, we stay with the core of the other person's message, but substitute a word here or there or change the sentence structure. Restatement is useful when the other person's message is clear and we wish to convey understanding, adding some variety. It is a good alternative to repetition, especially as our interaction unfolds:

OP: I called my pastor, and she said she'd stop by this afternoon. I have some things on my mind I need to tell her about.

H: You've asked your pastor to visit so you can talk over some concerns.

The helper's reflection is very similar to the other person's message, but not an exact match. She exchanges *"called my pastor and she said she'd stop by"* with *"asked your pastor to visit."* The helper could be mistaken. The person she is helping may not have expressly asked the pastor to come in—the pastor could have volunteered to do so during their phone conversation—but the exchange is close enough to reflect the core of the his message. Even if he corrects the caregiver—*"No, I didn't ask. She volunteered."*—the helper is in the ballpark and communicates her attention.

The loosest form of reflection comes through *paraphrase*: We put another person's message into our own words. Paraphrase is useful when the other person says a lot at one time or after we have used reflection and restatement and wish to pull together and highlight key thoughts. Good paraphrasing should be shorter and more concise than the original message:

OP: I'm really worried about what's happening with my kids. My sister is taking care of them. I can't seem to reach her, and she hasn't called. I don't know if everything is all right or not. She's usually not so out of touch. Maybe there's a problem she doesn't want to tell me about.
H: It's hard to know what's going on at home. Your sister usually keeps you up to date, and you're worried because you haven't heard from her.

This exchange could also look like the following:

OP: I'm really worried about what's happening with my kids.
H: You're worried about what's happening. [repetition]
OP: Yeah, my sister is taking care of them. I can't seem to reach her, and she hasn't called. I don't know if everything is all right or not.

H: You haven't been able to reach your sister and find out if everything is OK. [restatement]
OP: She's usually not so out of touch. Maybe there's a problem she doesn't want to tell me about.
H: It's hard to know what's going on at home. Your sister usually keeps you up to date, and you're worried because you haven't heard from her. [paraphrase]

After reflecting and restating the person's initial messages, the helper paraphrases all the main points. This use of paraphrase summarizes what has been said and paves the way for further communication.

A danger of paraphrase is the potential for changing meaning. Repetition and restatement keep us close to the other person's message and his perspective. When we paraphrase a message, putting it into our own words, we use our own mental and emotional filters and may come from our own point of view rather than the other person's. If this happens, distortion, judgment and/or interpretation may creep into the reflection.

OP: I met with the hospice people today. They say there is a bed available, and my daughter wants me to go because she can't really take care of me at home.
H: Your daughter would like to see you take advantage of this opportunity to go into hospice. It's a burden for her to manage your care.

The helper changes *"can't take care of me"* to *"burden."* It's a risky move. On the one hand, her turn of phrase may be right on the mark:

OP (with a sigh and sad tone): Yes, I feel like a burden to her. She has her own life to live. I don't want to interfere with that.

The helper's paraphrase has enabled the other person to move a bit deeper into his concern and communicate some of the feelings beneath the content.

On the other hand, the helper's choice of the word *"burden"* may be so far off target that the other person feels misunderstood:

> ***OP*** *(with offense): A burden? I don't think anyone in our family would consider it a burden to care for one of us! We take care of our own, and I'm not a burden or a bother to her.*

The other person's belief is that taking care of one another is part of being a family. The helper's suggestion that he might be a burden is offensive. Her paraphrase distorts the other person's message and disrupts the empathic connection. The other person feels misunderstood and may stop sharing his thoughts with the helper.

Judgment is another possible pitfall when we use paraphrase.

> ***OP:*** *My bad back keeps me from doing all the things I used to do. I wish my family would help me out more.*
> ***H:*** *They should know you can't do everything yourself. Your family is being insensitive not to help.*

The other person's family may be insensitive, but he hasn't said that. In this instance, the helper is labeling the family's behavior from her own value system. The other person may share this value system and agree with the helper:

> ***OP:*** *Insensitive? That's for sure! They don't understand at all.*

On the other hand, his family's behavior may not be what is on his mind:

OP: Insensitive? They care a lot about me!

The other person objects to the helper's judgment of his family. Because the empathic connection has been interrupted, he may not share what's really of concern to him. He might have been able to do so had the helper chosen to paraphrase in another way:

OP: My bad back keeps me from doing all the things I used to do. I wish my family would help out more.
H: You'd like it if your family did some of the things you can't do anymore because of your back.
OP: Yeah. But I hate asking for help. It makes me feel so dependent.
H: It's difficult to ask for help and to depend on your family to do things you used to be able to do.
OP: I feel so old and decrepit. I used to be so independent, and now I'm just falling apart all over the place. What's going to happen next?

Because of the helper's gentle, judgment-free, and more accurate paraphrases, the person with whom she is working is able to share more.

In spite of these pitfalls, paraphrase is a very effective tool for building the kind of relationship in which other healing work can take place. Repetition and restatement allow the other person's messages to unfold slowly. We give the other person time to form his thoughts and the opportunity to tell us what he is thinking and feeling a little at a time.

At other times, we may sense that the other person is ready to move more quickly through his message or that he needs help focusing on what is most important about what he is telling us. In that case, paraphrase is may be more useful than repetition or restatement.

As you become comfortable using reflection skills, you will find that the lines between repetition, restatement, and paraphrase begin to blur, and the three kinds of reflection blend together. For example:

OP: I have to have another test today.

H: Another test? [repetition]

OP: Yup. I hope it won't take long.

H: You hope it won't take long to do this test. [repetition]

OP: I really want to go home. I miss my cats a whole lot and I can't wait to see them.

H: You miss your cats and like the idea of going home because you'll be able to see them. [repetition—restatement]

OP: They mean a lot to me. My kids live too far away to visit often, so the cats keep me company, especially during the lonely times.

H: The cats provide some companionship when you get lonely. [restatement]

OP: I don't know what I'd do without them to fuss over.

H: In addition to keeping you company, they give you something to take care of. [restatement—paraphrase]

OP: They take care of me, too. Maybe it's just because I feed them, but they are all over me when I'm home. I think they know I love them, and they love me back.

H: So it would be very nice if this test didn't take too long so that you can get home and let your cats make a fuss over you. [paraphrase]

The helper's mix of paraphrase with repetition and restatement prompts the other person to talk about his concerns and moves their interaction forward in an empathic way.

Levels of Reflection

One of the choices we have to make when we reflect is deciding what to reflect. Sometimes the choice is easy. The other person's message is short, or the key point is very obvious. At other times deciding what to reflect is more difficult because the message is complex. We cannot reflect everything all the time, so we need to choose where to go.

Since messages have three components—content, feeling, and meaning—we can choose to reflect on any one of these. Often, one flows to the next. We touch the content, then the feeling, then the meaning of the other person's messages.

Reflection of *content* usually rests on the concrete facts of the story:

OP: I took three steps without my walker today!
H: Three steps...

The helper repeats part of the story. She might also have responded with restatement:

H: You didn't need to use your walker for three steps.

Reflection of feeling involves repeating, restating, or paraphrasing what the other person has said about his feelings or putting words to an emotion that is evident in his expression or in how he has said what he said:

OP (excitedly): Not having to use my walker is such a big deal. There was a time I wasn't sure I'd be able to do it.
H: You're pretty excited about this accomplishment. You were worried that you might never be able to walk without your walker and you did it.

The helper hears and reflects the other person's excitement. She follows this up with a restatement of the rest of the message, putting the spotlight on the worry that seems to be present in what he says.

Reflection of *meaning* involves highlighting the expressed or implied meaning of an event.

OP: I am excited. I was so afraid I'd be tied to the walker for the rest of my life and not be able to do anything that involved a lot of moving about. Now I know there is some hope.
H: Taking three steps is important because it means you can leave your

fears as well as your walker behind. That gives you hope.

When we address meaning, we reflect the importance of the event to the other person. The helper recognizes that the three steps the other person took are meaningful to him because he can move beyond his fears and have hope for the future.

When you are learning to reflect meaning, you may find it helpful to use the word "important" in your reflection. This keeps the focus on meaning and brings it to center stage for the other person. Reflection of meaning often includes a "because" phrase. Something (for example, walking without a walker) is important *because* it means something more to the patient (in this case, hope for a future that includes activity). If the "because" is clear in what the other person says you can include it in your reflection:

OP: My granddaughter is graduating from college today.

H: Wow, she's graduating! [repetition of content]

OP: Yes, isn't that great? I wish I could be there.

H: You'd like to celebrate with her. [restatement content and feeling]

OP: I never got to go to college, and neither did her mother. She is my only grandchild, and I'm so proud of her.

H: Her achievement is a real treat for you because she's been able to do something exceptional in your family. [reflection of meaning—what is important to the other person]

OP: I'm thrilled to be around to see her reach her dreams. I just wish I could be around there instead of here.

H: You're happy to know she's come so far. It would be even nicer for you if you could be there in person because she is important to you, and this is her special day. [reflection of meaning]

If the reason something is important isn't clear, leaving out the "because" is usually the best course of action. The other person may have many reasons why he finds the matter important, or he might not know what the meaning is. In these cases, we are in the position of guessing, and guessing comes from our own filters:

> *OP: I want to start painting again.*
> *H: Painting...?*
> *OP: Yes, I love to paint, and I haven't done it since my wife died. Painting is the way I express myself.*
> *H: You love painting, and you want to get back to it because it means you are coming to terms with your grief.*

In this case, the other person has not told the helper what painting means to him. The helper knows about the grieving process, and she interprets the meaning for him based on her experience. But her "because" is so far off that the other person feels very misunderstood:

> *OP: You don't understand. I'm not even close to coming to terms with my grief. Sometimes I don't think I've even started really grieving.*

The helper could have reflected meaning another way with better results:

> *OP: Yes, I love to paint, and I haven't done it since my wife died. Painting is the way I express myself.*
> *H: Painting to express yourself is important to you.*

Until we become skilled at reflecting meaning, sticking to noticing what the other person tells us and realizing that what he is telling us is important to him in some way is enough. Simply reflecting that something is important is reflection of meaning. We don't need to venture into the reasons why.

A Word of Caution

Reflection may seem like a very simple skill. It is. It also is powerful because it shows a person to himself. He hears what he has said, verbally and nonverbally, about what is happening, what he is feeling, and what is important to him. When we truly hear ourselves through the ears of others, we may begin to understand more about our experience. We may gain insight into something we have not previously known because of another's reflection of our message. We may be stimulated to go into a deeper exploration of these ideas. We probably will feel support, empathy, and understanding—qualities that are frequently rare in today's world.

Because of the trust and other relationship dynamics that characterize a helping relationship, people with whom we work who encounter these same experiences may feel safe and comfortable to go beyond what they might normally say to another person. Helpers who are not trained counselors need to be aware of the potential for getting into deep water and working beyond their limits as they use reflection.

It's a dilemma: We need to build the empathic connection to be able to help others in our primary work. We also need to be aware that through building that connection, we are weaving a safety net that may encourage the other person to disclose more than we wish we knew and are able to handle. Good reflection involves mirroring back what we see and hear. The further we move away from reflection and into paraphrase, the more we operate on our intuition, hunches, and own point of view. We also come closer to issues that are beneath his concern.

One of the axioms in helping is "don't dive into deep water if you don't know how to swim." As non-counseling helpers, we probably do not know how to swim in the deep water of facilitating insight and emotional release. Even if we do, our job is not to go there. Reaching underneath what the other person says to explore what he leaves unsaid is not within the scope of our work and is beyond limits of our competence.

A Word of Encouragement

After the word of caution, you may be tempted to forego the use of reflection. Please don't. Reflection is a fundamental skill in the helping encounter, one you may find yourself using more often than any other response. You—and those with whom you work—will benefit considerably from the empathy that grows from hearing and understanding what is said. Your helping relationships will be stronger and more supportive if you use repetition, restatement, and good paraphrase to reflect content and expressed feeling and meaning in your interactions with others. Keep it simple; stay close to the message; and above all, be fully present in empathy.

CHAPTER 5
Responding

Reflection is a powerful tool that is often all we need to sustain a helping interaction, especially when the person we are helping is open, forthcoming, and talkative. In these cases, our reflection keeps the other person talking because he feels understood and validated as he discloses what he has to say. Many occasions, however, call for us to go beyond reflection and respond to what the other person has said. This occurs when the other person stops short or seems to need a prompt to say more, or when we want to focus or direct a conversation.

Response differs from reflection in that it comes from us, not the other person. It is our message *in response to* his message. Good responses follow reflection. The other person's disclosure, helper reflection, further disclosure, and further response flow in cyclical or spiral pattern. This example illustrates one way these processes might work:

OP: Ah...it's good to be here today.
H: You're glad to be here. [reflection]
OP: I really like massage.
H: You like it, eh? [reflection]
OP: Yeah. I think it's very helpful.
H: Me, too. I certainly benefit when I'm on the receiving end. I feel so much more relaxed. [response]
OP: That goes for me, too.
H: You certainly seem more relaxed to me—and it feels like there is much less tension in your left shoulder. What does it feel like to you? [response]
OP: I think that's true. It certainly doesn't hurt as much.
H: There's less pain. [reflection]

OP: And I'm able to sleep better at night.
H: All the things you are noticing go together. Massage can improve sleep because it reduces tension and pain. [response]
OP: Whatever is happening, I like it.
H: You like all the benefits. [reflection]

In this example, the helper goes back and forth between reflection and response. Her reflection acknowledges and validates what the other person has said, and her response adds new material. Notice that reflection is at least as prevalent as response in this exchange. The helper moves in and out of supporting the other person's experience as she shares her own perspective. In this way, she continues to be empathic and there for the other person, and she becomes more of an active party in the exchange.

This example also illustrates three ways in which we can respond to another person's message. We can disclose something about ourselves (*self-disclosure*); we can share our perception of the other person (*feedback*); and we can comment on the situation (*information giving*). In her first response to the person with whom she is working, the helper briefly and generally discloses the fact that massage benefits her, too, and she joins with the other person in the experience of enjoying massage. This prompts the other person to provide more details about how treatment is benefiting him. Next, the helper gives the other person feedback, telling him how she experiences him and checking her perception by asking what he experiences. She then provides information about massage based on her professional expertise and relates it to the other person's situation.

Response can also occur non-verbally, through silence, movement, and touch. A non-verbal response sometimes is the best thing to offer. There simply isn't anything we can say that would further the discussion, especially when the realities of a situation—the other person's feelings, experiences, or circumstances—are painful:

OP (sadly): The doctor told me my grandfather's cancer is very advanced.
H: It's advanced. [reflection]
OP: Yes. I know he is going to die soon.
H: Hmmm… (silence). [response]

At this point, it might be appropriate for the helper to touch the other person's hand or nod her head gently in resonance with the other person's understanding of the gravity or sadness of the situation. By using a nonverbal response, the helper stands as a silent witness to the other person's experience.

Responding Through Self-Disclosure

As the term implies, self-disclosure is the process of disclosing something about ourselves. When we talk about ourselves and tell someone else what we are thinking, feeling, or experiencing in the present moment or share relevant information about our lives, we reveal who we are as a person.

OP: Thanks for the Reiki. These sessions really make my day.
H: I'm glad. I enjoy working with you.

OP: I'm thrilled about the improvements I'm noticing.
H: Me, too. It's exciting for me to see the changes in your ability to move about.

OP: It seems like there are big holes in my life now that my son is married. I don't know what to do with myself.
H: There are times when I've found loneliness a difficult thing to manage.

The responses to these messages are about the helper. In the context of these conversations, the helper tells the other person how she feels and what she experiences. Her disclosures are short and related to what the other person is saying. Her purpose in using self-disclosure is not go on at length or into detail about her life, but to provide enough of her reality to be a person who is more than the role she plays as a helper.

It should go without saying that anything we disclose about ourselves should be true. People generally know when they are hearing something untrue. Making something up about ourselves simply for the purpose of saying "me, too." is patronizing, unethical, inauthentic (not genuine), and potentially harmful to the empathic connection.

Some core emotional experiences are part of the human condition—loss, joy, love, fear, sorrow, guilt, etc. We all have them in one form or another, to one extent or another, at some time during our lives. These experiences come in many forms. Loss, for example, occurs with any change, especially those in which we feel we are not getting something in return—death, disability, divorce, disappointment, etc. The *circumstances* of loss may be unique to us, but the *experience* of loss is shared. We feel angry and sad and lost, and we long for things to go back to the way they were before we are able to find meaning in the event and integrate it into our lives. We know what it is like to want to keep the moment alive forever when we are full of joy and love. Thus, at the emotional level, we can identify with almost everything others experience. Our identification is with the shared aspects of these emotional experiences, rather than with the personal details.

> *OP: My dad fell last night, and he lay on the floor all night because he couldn't get to the phone. I didn't find him until I went over this morning. I feel awful about this.*
> *H: It is hard for you to know you weren't there to help him at the time.* [reflection]
> *OP: Yes. I feel really guilty about not being there. At the same time, I feel really angry that he hasn't listened to me about the danger of living on his own. I worry about him because I can't help when I'm not there, but I can't be there all the time.*
> *H: I've not been in this same situation, but I know how difficult it is for me when I need to take care of things and can't do it all. I feel very out of control. Is it like this for you?* [response]

The helper has never encountered the same situation at the level of content, and she shares that fact. But what is the other person's core experience? Guilt; anger; worry; feeling out of control—emotional events that most of us have experienced. The helper discloses what it's like for her to be caught in the dilemma of wanting to do something and not being able to do it. She names it for herself as feeling *"out of control."*

In this example, the helper also does something else. Since she is extracting the universal experience from the details provided by the other person and disclosing what she perceives to be a similar experience, she checks to see if she has named an experience in line with what the other person feels and returns the focus of the exchange to the other person.

Boundaries

In the first chapter, we looked at the ways in which healing relationships are different from friendships. Unlike friendship, which is usually a two-way street, the healing relationship is primarily a one-way street. We may benefit from our healing encounters with others, but what matters is the benefit to the other person. A boundary is between us, a place where we end and the other person begins. As helpers, we must respect that boundary and avoid crossing it with too much or the wrong kind of self-disclosure.

The danger of self-disclosure centers on the potential for flooding the helping encounter with information about ourselves that is inappropriate, irrelevant, and potentially harmful to us and to the other person in a relationship. When we listen to others and witness their experiences, the relationship between us becomes closer. The sense of connection that develops can cause us to disclose more than what is helpful. When helpers share too much, especially too much personal information about ourselves, we cross the boundary between us and the other person.

OP: My nurse practitioner suggested that I might benefit from some energy work. I was raped about six months ago. She said I'm okay physically, and I've done all the counseling I can stand. But I'm still not right.

H (response #1): I know what that's like. My neighbor sexually abused me when I was a child, and it has taken years of treatment of all kinds to help me heal. Sometimes I wonder what more I can do to recover.

H (response #2): I know how long it can take us to heal from a trauma like rape.

Since the other person is coming for help, she has the need and right to tell the helper these things. What the helper does not have the need or right to do is to respond in the first way. Her trauma history is not an appropriate or necessary disclosure. Her experience is too personal and none of the other person's business. In the second response, the helper joins with the other person around *"length of time for healing"* rather than *"trauma history."* Her familiarity with the length of time it takes for the whole person to heal from trauma might have come from her own past or from her work with others; she doesn't say, nor should she.

Flooding of the boundary between us and the other people need not involve disclosure of very personal material. Consider the two different helper responses in this example:

OP: It's been a great day today. I was able to get up and fix my own breakfast. I haven't been able to do that in a long time.

H (response #1): I've had a good day, too, because I was able to get my son out the door, with his lunch and homework, and get to work on time. It's been such a struggle for me since his father left us. Trying to do everything all at once seems impossible, and every little success is really a big one. Getting to work on time is something I haven't been able to do on a regular basis since he started school last fall.

H (response #2): What a treat for you. It's always nice for me when I am able to do things today that I couldn't do before.

In the first response, the helper goes overboard by sharing too much of her own experience. She dumps too much information into the space between her and the other person. Most of the information is tangential to what the other person has said, and it occupies space that belongs to the person she is there to help. These are the kinds of things the helper might say to a friend, someone with whom she shares personal details, but they are comments that are inappropriate in a helping relationship.

In the second response, the helper reflects and joins with the other person with a generalized self-disclosure. Rather than revealing the details about how the day is a good one for her, the helper connects with the other person's experience of accomplishment and pleasure in doing something for himself by sharing that she feels the same way when this occurs in her own life. She knows what having a good day is like, so she can speak with genuineness. That's what counts—not the details of her story. Her disclosure is short, relevant, and helpful.

Stealing the Show

Self-disclosure highlights our experience. When we talk about ourselves, we take the spotlight off the other person and direct it our way. The benefit of this is the communication of a shared experience. The danger comes in continuing to focus on ourselves, rather than returning it to the other person.

Look at the difference between these two possible helper responses:

OP: I'm worried about how my kids will handle the news I'm getting married again. I'm afraid they are going to freak out.
H (response #1): Boy, I know what you mean about family members freaking out. My parents are going to be really upset when I tell them I'm giving up my own apartment to move in with my new partner.
H (response #2): It's a worry for you. I know it can be hard for my family members to accept big changes in my life. I'm wondering if that's true for you, too.

In the first response, the helper again says too much about herself and discloses material that is really of no benefit to the patient. She also puts the focus on herself and paves the way for the conversation to shut down or become unhelpful because it concerns the helper's situation, not the other person's.

In the second response, the helper reflects the other person's feeling of worry, and she discloses something general about her own experience that is related to the other person's circumstances. She refocuses the conversation on him after her brief self-disclosure by wondering if what she experienced is like his experience. In this way, the helper joins momentarily with the other person by revealing a similar experience and invites him to add to what he has said.

The helper moves up to the boundary between her and the other person, and then moves back to give him room to continue with his own concerns. I've found the best way to do this is through "wondering"— "I'm wondering if this is your experience, too," or "I wonder if this is how it is for you"—and through the use of a simple question: "Is that how it is for you?"

Presuming We Know

Checking out whether what we have disclosed relates to what the other person is experiencing is an important factor in using self-disclosure. If we presume our experience is like the other person's, we run the risk of weakening rather than strengthening the empathic connection with our self-disclosure.

> *OP: It's really difficult for me to admit my mother to hospice. It makes her coming death seem that much more real.*
> *H (response #1): I know how you feel.*
> *H (response #2): I know how you feel. I felt really sad when my mother needed more help than I could give her. You must feel this way, too.*
> *H (response #3): I had a very difficult time when my mother needed hospice help. I wonder how you feel.*

The first response, *"I know how you feel,"* is not empathic, because we can never know how someone else feels. This response is hollow and trite and a caricature of the helping exchange (as is *"I hear you"*). It is neither empathic nor helpful. The second response is somewhat better because the helper adds material to back up her presumption that she knows how the other person feels. By naming that feeling as *"sad"* and telling the other person he *"must"* feel that way, she runs the risk of describing the other person's experience inaccurately—even though she has just said she knows how he feels. This contradiction shakes—and potentially breaks—the empathic connection. The third response is the best of the three because the helper does not presume to know what the other person's experience is. More than that, after disclosing her own experience in general, she invites the other person to tell her how he feels.

Responding with Feedback

When we give feedback, we share our perspective of another person with that person. We tell him something we notice about him for the purpose of helping him better understand how he might be. Feedback is a description of what we observe and acts like a mirror in which the other person can consider himself from our perspective. What we say may be something he already knows, or it might be new information he can evaluate and use if he thinks it's valuable or discard if it's not. To a certain extent, responding with feedback can be considered a form of self-disclosure because we are disclosing what we see about another person, but the responses differ. In self-disclosure we are talking about *ourselves*; in feedback, we are sharing how we see the *other person*.

> *OP: I got another traffic ticket on the way in here. At the same place, too! I think the cops just sit around and wait for me to come down the road. I mean, yeah, I was going too fast, but he could have just given me a warning.*
> *H (response #1): I get really annoyed when I get caught and have to face the full consequences of doing something like that. Even if I've gotten away with it in the past, it never feels fair to me when I get caught.* [self-disclosure]
> *H (response #2): You have been very lucky in the past. Given the tone of your voice and look on your face right now, it seems to me that you're pretty mad at that cop for throwing the book at you this time around. Is that the case?* [feedback]

ANNE R. BEWLEY, PH.D.

The first helper responds with self-disclosure, relating her own experience. The second helper responds with feedback, sharing her observations of the other person.

Helpful Feedback

Many of the guidelines that pertain to self-disclosure are also applicable when giving feedback. Helpful feedback comes when we relate what is true in our experience, respect the boundary between the other person and us, and return control of the conversation to him. Other factors also contribute to making feedback useful to others.

Useful feedback is specific. A description of what someone is noticing about our behavior is much easier for us to work with than someone's overall impression of us. When we know what we are doing leads someone to an impression of us, we have an opportunity to observe ourselves and validate or clarify that impression.

> *OP: I'm not having much success with this weight loss thing.*
> *H (response #1): You seem discouraged.*
> *H (response #2): I notice that you're slouching in the chair. You are also frowning, and you just gave a big sigh. It looks to me like you might be pretty discouraged. I'm wondering how it feels from your side.*

In this example, the first helper tells the other person he *"seems discouraged."* The other person may not know how the helper gets that impression. The helper tells him he is slouching, scowling, and sighing, and that his behavior comes across to the helper as discouragement. The other person can use that specific information to check out his experience and identify how he "looks" to himself.

If he recognizes he is discouraged, he can acknowledge it. Or, if he realizes that he is worried about whether he is doing something wrong or concerned about a specific aspect of weight-related health, or preoccupied with a more pressing concern, he can correct the helper's impression—

especially since the helper has returned the focus to him and invited him to share what he is feeling.

Useful feedback accommodates the fact that what we see is filtered through perceptions and leaves open the possibility we are wrong. Our impression or experience of someone's behavior belongs to us, not them. What we see is not necessarily how the other person is, especially in his own mind.

Helpful feedback is expressed in terms of what could be possible, what might be true, what we see as a tendency, what seems apparent to us, etc. Feedback delivered as a statement of our experience of way things appear is more "hearable" than feedback delivered as the way things are. When we make it clear that what we are saying is how something seems or looks to us, we allow room for the possibility we are mistaken.

OP (with a sigh, frown, and complaining tone of voice): I can't believe you're here to make me do this again. I've tried and tried to button my shirt, and no amount of practice seems to help.
H (response #1): Your frown and tone of voice tell me you want to give up learning how to button your shirt.
H (response #2): By the frown on your face and the tone of your voice it seems to me you are discouraged and might want to give up.

The first helper tells the other person he is giving up. Her feedback sounds blunt, absolute, and potentially judgmental. If the helper's feedback is on the mark (the other person *is* giving up), it may not cause a problem. In fact, her feedback may give the other person a chance to recognize and admit that he is so discouraged he wants to quit trying. But if her feedback is not true, the other person can feel judged, shamed, or put down—and perhaps get defensive and contrary.

The second helper relates her perception (*"it seems to me"*) that the other person could possibly (*"might"*) want to give up. The other person can respond to the feedback in a number of ways. He can look at his experience through the eyes of the helper and agree or disagree without feeling judged. Or, he can identify a feeling along a continuum of wanting to give up, rather than having to choose between wanting and not wanting to give up. He is less likely to feel defensive.

Using phrases like "it seems (or looks) to me" before describing someone's behavior helps both helpers and the other person to keep in mind that we are talking about our perspective on the situation, not "the truth." Using words like "might" and "could" put what we see in the realm of possibility rather than reality.

Helpful feedback focuses on behavior, not personality. Behavior is something we can usually change, if we want to enough; for the most part, personality is not. When we think about what drives us nuts or what we love about another person, we usually discover is something he does: he leaves things lying around, he delays in calling us back, he jokes around, etc.

What we tend to do, however, is describe that person in terms of his behavior: He is a slob; he is a procrastinator: he is a clown. When we do this, we pigeonhole the other person, putting him in a category that excludes all other aspects of him.

OP: I know this is the umpteenth time, but let me try again.
H (response #1): I've seen you work very hard today. You're such a perfectionist!
H (response #2): I've seen you work very hard today. It seems to me that learning to do this perfectly is important to you. Is that the case?

Both helpers share their observation that the other person has worked hard. The first helper labels that behavior as the personality of the person himself: He is a perfectionist. The other person may be perfectionististic—but labeling him a perfectionist can be unwelcome, even if delivered with a smile or in a gently teasing way. By telling him he is a perfectionist, we give him little information about what he is doing to give us that impression, behaviors he might like and want to keep, or behaviors he might not like and want to change. The second helper leaves the other person's actions in the realm of behavior and shares her impression of the behavior—that doing things perfectly is important to the other person. Having an opportunity to look at the possibility that doing things perfectly is important to him—perhaps even too important—is likely to be of more value to the other person than being categorized by that behavior.

In order to be useful, feedback needs to be given in a way the other person can hear. We can easily get defensive when someone tells us how we appear in their eyes, especially if we think their comments are negative. Feedback is simply information; our perception about it makes it positive or negative. Many of us, however, find it difficult to listen to others' impression of us. We tend to be wary when someone gives us feedback. We need to keep this in mind when responding to others with what we perceive about them.

One of the ways to give helpful feedback is by using the "feedback sandwich." This consists of placing feedback that might be construed as negative by the other person between two positive statements. Consider how different these responses sound:

OP: This exercising thing is great. What a difference it makes.

H (response #1): You are very enthusiastic about the results. You have put a lot of effort into working your right arm and made good progress. Your left arm still seems a little weak, and it looks to me like you may have been neglecting it in your routine.

H (response #2): You are very enthusiastic about the results. Your left arm still seems little weak, and it looks to me like you may have been neglecting it in your routine. On the other hand, you have put a lot of effort into working your right arm and made good progress.

The helper in response #1 begins with the "good news" and ends with the "bad news." By leaving the bad news for last, the helper stresses what the other person is not doing well. This response would be even less helpful if it included the word "but:" *"You have put a lot of effort into working your right arm and made good progress. But your left arm still seems little week...."* The word "but" tends to negate anything that comes before, so the other person does not hear the good news.

The helper in response #2 sandwiches the bad news between two pieces of good news. The other person is much more likely to hear the second response than the first, because the first and last things he hears are what is good about what he is doing.

Helpful feedback never includes sarcasm. Sometimes sarcasm comes as praise in the form of a putdown. For example:

OP: I thought I did pretty well that time.
H: Oh, I don't know. Are you sure you've done it enough to get it right?

A positive message underlies the helper's negative remark, and that is the one the other person is supposed to hear: *You certainly did!* The helper's reply is not so bad if she and the other person have an understanding that lets him hear the real message. But the reality is that sarcasm is cutting humor, and it can hurt. If we want to say something positive about the other person, we are more helpful (and empathic) if we say it directly. If we need to say something critical, doing so without sarcasm is kinder and more empathic. Sarcasm is best left out of interaction with others.

Helpful feedback is delivered for the benefit of the other person, not ourselves. The point is to help the other person see something about himself that he may not know, not for us to get in our digs or meet our own needs. Giving feedback under the guise of "being honest" or for our own purposes—being superior, being right, getting back at someone, etc.—is not helpful. This kind of feedback sounds very judgmental:

OP: I thought I did pretty well that time.
H (response #1): It was better, but you still don't have it right. Besides that, you're not putting a lot of effort into this. You can't do it with your hand in that position.

The helper comes across as critical and may be responding out of a need of her own, rather than for the benefit of the other person. It could be that the other person is not doing it right or putting enough effort into his attempts. However, holding someone to a standard is one thing; criticizing him for not measuring up is another. Our job is to be helpful, not hurtful. In this case, the helper can give feedback in better ways. Compare these possible responses:

OP: I thought I did pretty well that time.
H (response #2): You did, and you can do it right with more of the

same kind of effort you are putting into this.
H (response #3): *Yes, you're getting better at this. You might want to try it again with just a little more oomph. If you turn your hand in this direction, you could be more successful.*

Response #2 acknowledges what is good in realistic terms and addresses the other person's apparent lack of effort with encouragement and a positive correction. The helper gives him room for making choices about whether he wants to try again, put more effort into his attempt, and correct his approach. The third response included specific information about how to improve. The helper's intent is to provide the other person with accurate, specific feedback in a supportive and genuine way.

Responding to Mixed Messages

Good responses to mixed messages happen by way feedback. When we notice two messages that conflict—often a verbal and a nonverbal message, we direct our response in a way that helps the other person reflect on and clarify what he is saying. For example:

OP (with an anxious tone): *This is a big day. I find out whether I was accepted into the program I applied to. It's no big deal if I don't make it, though, so I'm not worried about it.*
H: *On the one hand, you are saying that it's a big day, and the tone of your voice sounds like you might feel anxious. On the other hand, you're telling me it's no big deal and you're not worried.*
OP (reply #1): *Yeah...I guess it really does matter, and I will be on pins and needles until I hear. I like to pretend it doesn't matter, just in case I get bad news, but it really does.*
OP (reply #2): *Yeah...I guess I'm both anxious and not anxious. It's like I care, but in a way I don't care. I'd like to be accepted, but if I don't, I'll still be OK. I have other options.*

The helper points out both sides of the message, giving the other person a chance to see the discrepancy in what he is saying. Because of the helper's feedback, the other person more directly addresses his experience. In the first reply, he reveals that he really is anxious and identifies his saying that it doesn't matter what happens as a cover-up for his anxiety. In the second reply, the other person admits that he feels two ways at once. Both replies show how the other person can become more honest with himself and with us when he has an opportunity to hear feedback.

The technique the helper used to give feedback is a useful approach to addressing double messages. She divides the mixed message into its component parts. *"On the one hand"* lies one part of the message (that this situation is a big deal and he's anxious); *"on the other hand"* lies the second part of the message (that he is suggesting it is not a big deal and he's not concerned). In this way, she shows the other person that he has two coexisting experiences and invites him to explore them both. What the helper does not do is assume that one or the other messages is the right one. She uses feedback to help the other person tell her what is true about his experience, rather than risking misunderstanding by determining this for herself.

Providing Information

When we respond with self-disclosure, we share our own experience. When we respond with feedback, we share our experience of the other person. A third response involves providing information that is relevant and helpful to the situation.

OP: I seem to be stronger today than yesterday.
H: I agree. These exercises work the muscles in your leg than were affected by your stroke. Doing the other set regularly will continue to build your strength.

The helper speaks from her knowledge and experience and tells the other person more about what is happening in their work together.

OP: I don't understand why my wife's surgery has been delayed. Is there a problem with the insurance paperwork?
H: The paperwork is just fine. The schedule has been pushed back because of an emergency. Right now, it looks like she will go down to the operating room about noon.

The helper answers the other person's question and briefly explains the facts of the situation.

Providing information does not mean talking out of turn, however, and helpers must be sure that what they are saying is within the scope of their work and relevant to the other person. Spreading gossip is not professional or helpful.

OP: I don't understand why my wife's surgery has been delayed. Is there a problem with the insurance paperwork?
H: No, it's not about that. You see, there was a horrible accident on the highway, and two people were critically injured. The emergency medical team couldn't get its act together to get there fast enough. Personally, I don't know why the hospital even uses that ambulance company any more. I don't think they have a clue about how to respond to emergencies. The surgeon is the kind of doc you don't want to upset— I know from experience—and she was really angry at them, because she had to rush into surgery. That has pushed back the schedule. It'll take the morning to sort out that mess. I imagine your wife will go down to the operating room about noon.

It may be helpful for the other person to know in general why his wife's surgery has been delayed, but he should be spared the helper's gossip, critical commentary, and personal opinion and given only information he has a need or right to know.

The information we provide should be based in fact, not on what the helper thinks might be the case. When a helper doesn't know something, she should admit it—and find out, if she can.

> OP: *I don't understand why my wife's surgery has been delayed. Is there a problem with the insurance paperwork?*
> H *(response #1): I don't know for sure, but I think the paperwork problem is solved. I guess an emergency or something else came up to push back the schedule. Your wife will probably go down to the operating room early this afternoon.*
> H *(response #2): The paperwork problem is solved. I don't know what the delay is all about. I'll go see if I can get a reliable estimate of what the new surgery timetable is and when the folks in the operating room think they'll be ready for your wife.*

The first helper's response is based on what she thinks or guesses, rather than what she knows. She is making up information. The second helper tells the other person what she knows, and she is willing to find out what she doesn't know so that she can provide information based on facts, not hunches.

In addition to being sure that information is correct, within the other person's need and right to know, and based in fact rather than opinion, we need to be aware of the potential for our being perceived as patronizing. This can happen when we state the obvious or talk down to the other person from our professional position.

> OP: *I don't understand why my wife's surgery has been delayed. Is there a problem with her insurance paperwork?*
> H: *This sort of thing happens all the time in hospitals, you know. There has to be a good reason for the delay. Everyone scheduled by surgery has been affected, and your wife will just have to wait her turn, like everyone else.*

The helper's comment is not particularly informative, nor does it communicate respect for the other person's desire to understand the reason for the delay. When we talk down to others, we run the risk of lecturing, moralizing, or preaching, none of which are helpful ways to provide information because they are laden with "lessons," value statements, and judgment. In the last example, the helper lectures the other person about what he needs to do to manage the situation and preaches a lesson in turn taking.

A final challenge to be aware of is the fact that information giving can serve as a disguise for giving advice. Advice is not particularly helpful unless you are in the role of advisor. Even then, we can find ways to help others come to their own conclusions about what to do that are more helpful than telling them what they should do. When we are asked for advice, we usually better serve the other person by reflecting his concern than by responding with information or by asking him a question (next chapter).

When Response is Not Helpful

Sometimes, no response is wise or helpful. We helpers need to be ready, willing, and able to respond from a centered place, and the other person needs to be ready, willing, and able to receive our response. One of the key obstacles to giving and receiving a good response is strong emotion.

When we are angry, upset, or emotionally "hooked" by what the other person has said, we are out of balance emotionally and cannot respond from a place of clarity and centeredness. This is a problem in helping relationships because the power in the relationship is unequally distributed. Regardless of the setting or our intention, we as helpers are in the position of greater influence. Any emotionally fueled or defensive response we make is likely to have a much stronger effect in a helping encounter than in a personal relationship because we are in a position of authority.

One of the things that can draw us into giving an unhelpful response is being the target for someone else's anger. When this happens, our first reaction is likely to be a desire to defend ourselves. We are tempted to strike back:

> **OP** *(clearly angry): I told the nurse I don't want any visitors today, and you come barging in. Get out!*
> **H:** *Hey, don't yell at me. The nurse didn't tell me. Given your mood today, I'm happy to leave.*

The helper's response is full of blame and judgment, as well as a lack of accountability (it's the nurse's fault the helper didn't know). A far better response at a time like this is self-disclosure in which the helper acknowledges what she is feeling, rather than sharing her perspective of the other person:

> **OP** *(clearly angry): I told the nurse I don't want any visitors today, and you come barging in. Get out!*
> **H:** *I apologize for disturbing you. I didn't get the word. If would like a visit later, please let me know. I'll be here all afternoon.*

The helper uses self-disclosure and owns her part of the experience. She also lets the other person know that his anger has not affected her willingness to continue to help.

The people with whom we work are often people who are in physical, emotional, or social pain. Because of their problems, they hurt, and they may deal with their feelings by attacking us when we offer to help. At the same time, they are very afraid that their anger will cause us to withdraw our help and leave them alone.

For example, the adolescent who is angry about not being able to go to the mall may scream at his mother, telling her to get out of his face. He may want her to leave his presence. Her doing so gives him some power in this situation, even if he can't go to the mall, but he doesn't want her to leave for good. At the same time, he is afraid she will because he has lashed out at her. The mother's most helpful and loving response at a time like this is to tell him, in some way, that she will get out of his face and that she is still nearby.

Adults are the same as this teen-ager. When they are in pain or other distress they can push us away at the same time they want us to stay present in their lives. What they say to us may be what they want in the short run but contradict what they want in the long run. If we respond in a way that gives them what they ask for in the moment and assure them we are not abandoning them, we keep the empathic connection.

An example of this kind of non-defensive, accepting response comes from the experience of a friend of mine whose coworker had just learned that his cancer was in the final stage and that he did not have long to live:

H: Would you like to talk about this?

OP: (with sarcasm and anger) Now that's a happy topic. Thanks a lot! Why would I want to talk about it?

H: I won't mention it again. I just want you to know that this is something I have experience with, and that I am here if you ever do want to talk.

It must have been difficult for her to stay in such a centered place when her initial offer to help was so roughly rebuffed. But she did not let the other person's anger throw her off. She indicated that she respected his desire not to talk (*"I won't mention it again."*) and let him know she was still willing to be part of his experience if he so chose. (By the way, he never said anything about his impending death again, but my friend sensed he was more comfortable around her than he was around other coworkers during his last weeks at work.)

When emotion other than anger floods the person with whom we are working the other person may be incapable of making good use of what we have to say. The emotional waves must pass over and through him first. Then he may be ready to listen.

OP (bursting into tears): I can't believe she's gone.

H (response #1): I find it hard to believe, too, and I feel sad for your loss.
H (response #2): You are crying very hard and are very upset.
H (response #3): Hmmm...(silence).

All three responses address the other person's experience. The first is in the form of self-disclosure: The helper is telling the other person how she feels. At this point, the other person probably doesn't care. He needs to feel his emotions first, and then he might be interested in how his situation makes the helper feel. The second response is feedback. The helper is telling the other person what she observes about him. He probably already knows that he is crying, so her comments are not particularly helpful. The helper also sounds very detached as she describes what she sees. Her feedback is accurate, but her response lacks empathy. The third response is a gently introduced silence. The helper makes a sound to acknowledge that she has heard him, and then she gives him room to cry. The other person's tears will come to an end (for the time being), and then he and the helper may be able to talk about his experience.

Because helpers work to make things better for other people, we can feel helpless when nothing we can do or say will help. Watching people struggle with problems or suffer emotionally or physically is disheartening, and we can fall into the trap of reassuring them to make ourselves feel better about our inability to help. Wanting to make things better this way is particularly a problem when we are working with children. We are accustomed to consoling them with comments like, *"There's nothing to worry about."*

OP: I miss my dad. I hope he's OK.
H: Don't be upset. There's nothing to worry about.

The helper's response takes away or minimizes the other person's experience and denies him the right to feel the way he does. The other person is worried; the helper tells him not to be. Now he's worried and wrong for worrying! The helper also assures him that there is nothing to worry about, something she cannot be sure about.

One of the least helpful responses we can give others is a statement based in our beliefs about life:

OP: This is the most difficult situation I've ever experienced.
H: I'm sure things will come out right. Everything happens for a reason. God probably has a higher purpose in mind for you.

The helper responds from her own philosophy and religion. The helper's response might be helpful if the other person shares her point of view and the setting in which they are working is appropriate for talking about religious belief. However, her response is very likely to break the empathic connection between her and the other person if he has a different belief system. Unless we are sure we have a philosophy of life and religious beliefs in common, we are on shaky ground sharing our thoughts in this regard. In this case, the helper would have expressed more care by reflecting and encouraging the other person to talk about what he believed about this situation than imposing her point of view.

Who Benefits?

When it comes to responding in a healing encounter, we must keep in mind the question of who benefits from our saying what we think, feel, and see. In other words, what we as helpers do should serve to build the empathic connection and support the other person. It might seem obvious that this should be the case, but unfortunately, because of the dynamics of the helping relationship, some care providers can operate out of self-interest or the need to feed their own egos rather than the interest of those they are helping.

Before responding beyond reflection, we should stop, look, and choose what to say or do with care. By pausing briefly, we have an opportunity to view the other person and his message and sense the best way to respond. If what we are about to say will benefit the other person and our healing relationship, we are on steady ground.

CHAPTER 6
Asking Questions

Reflecting and responding are skills in which we make statements about what we are hearing from another person, disclose information about ourselves, offer feedback, and provide information. Up to this point, we have not talked about asking questions. I have left them for last because I find questions to be among the least helpful helping interventions unless they are well formed, well timed, and well asked. A more effective way to accomplish the intent behind a desire to ask a questions almost always exists. By using reflection or response, we can achieve a better result in terms of deepening the empathic connection and encouraging the other person to express his concerns than we can by asking a question.

> *OP: I really miss my son. I wish he'd come to visit.*
> *H: How long has it been since you've seen him?*
> *OP: Only about three weeks, but I still miss him.*
> *H: Are you and your son close?*
> *OP: Yes.*
> *H: How often do you usually see him?*
> *OP: Twice a week.*
> *H: Have you talked to him on the phone?*
> *OP: Yes.*

The helper wants to communicate her interest in the other person, but her use of questions gradually reduces the depth and substance of their interaction. What she asks about is not what is important to the other person. Moreover, she misses what *does* matter to him. The helping conversation drifts away from the other person's experience into information about the circumstances surrounding his concern. So, rather than communicating interest and stimulating the other person's expression, the helper weakens the empathic relationship with her questions.

Look at how reflection and response accomplish the helper's goals in ways that build the empathic connection:

OP: I really miss my son. I wish he'd come to visit.

H: You'd like to see your son.

OP: Yes, I would. I haven't seen him in a long time.

H: A long time...

OP: Well, about three weeks. But I usually see him a couple of times a week.

H: It sounds to me like seeing him is pretty important to you.

OP: Yes, we're very close.

H: So it's hard for you when you don't get to see him on a regular basis.

OP: It is, indeed. But we talked on the phone, and he said he might be in tomorrow. I sure hope so.

H: It would be nice for you to see him tomorrow.

These possible helper responses are likely to prompt the other person to say more about his son and his feeling of missing him and his wish he would come visit. They are better than questions because they deepen the level of communication and result in the other person saying more. He has had the opportunity to express his thoughts and feelings in his own way and on his own time, rather than according to the structure provided by the helper's questions. He provides all the information the first helper asked for, but the quality of the interaction is richer.

Questions do have a place in healing interaction. They are effective when reflection and response no longer work to move the other person forward. Every theme has a natural resting point or conclusion; the conversation stops and needs a nudge if we wish to continue our interaction. Questions become useful as nudges. They can focus or deepen where we are already going, or they can steer the interaction in a new direction.

> *OP: I feel great today!*
> *H: You're feeling great.* [reflection]
> *OP: Yes. I've had wonderful news about my daughter.*
> *H: Good news always makes me feel good.* [response—self-disclosure]
> *OP: Yeah. She got into the college she wanted.*
> *H: That is good news.*
> *OP: Sure is.*

At this point, the interaction has come to a natural pause, and the helper has a couple of choices. She can ask a good question to invite the other person to say more about this topic, or she can use a good question to steer the interaction in another direction:

> *H: That is good news.*
> *OP: Sure is.*
> *H (question #1): What else is good today?*
> *H (question #2): What else is up with you today?*
> *H (question #3): Are you ready to hop up on the table for your treatment?*
> *H (question #4): How did you do with your exercises this week?*

The first two questions invite the other person to say more about feeling good. The second two questions consider the pause in the interaction a sign that the other person has finished, and they help the helper direct the interaction to something else.

Kinds of Questions

Two different kinds of questions are used in the previous example, closed and open. The third question is a closed question; the others are open. Closed questions have a specific purpose. They limit the number of logical responses the other person has and force a choice between "yes" and "no." Closed questions also have a time and place in which they may be the best course of action. When a person is not able to respond verbally, for example, their speech is impaired, they have had a stroke, or they are on a ventilator, they cannot give us much information. They can respond, however, to either/or choices and yes/no questions.

We also ask closed questions when we want a yes or no answer, often in order to decide what to do or where next to go with the interaction. In this example, the helper simply wants to know if the other person is ready for her treatment.

H: Are you ready to hop up on the table for your treatment?
OP (reply #2): Sure.
OP (reply #2): Not quite. I need to ask you about something that happened this week.

Closed questions usually begin with a "are you,' "were you," "will you be," "have you," "can/could/would/should you," or "did you":

Are you in pain?
Do you have any pain?
Will you be discharged today?
Are you finished with your lunch?
Were you successful in completing that assignment?
Will you be taking care of your partner?

Notice that "you" is the second word in each of these questions. This is almost a sure-fire way to identify a closed question. These questions can be answered with a "yes" or "no." The other person can stop there, without giving any further information. When that happens, we can get into a pattern of interrogation in which we ask closed question after closed question, reaping little reward for our effort:

> *H: Will you be taking care of your partner?*
> *OP: Yes.*
> *H: Are you planning on getting some help with his care?*
> *OP: No.*
> *H: Can you manage on your own?*
> *OP: Yes.*

The helper gained little information through her use of questions. Her questions seem based on her desire for information, not her interest in helping the other person. Her intent may be to get into the helping part after she has the necessary information, but she could get what she needs and help develop the interaction by using reflection to invite the other person to tell her more.

Further caution should be considered before using closed questions: Closed questions often hide suggestions, judgment, or advice that is not helpful to the other person:

> *H: Will you be taking care of your partner?*
> *OP: Yes.*
> *H: Have you thought about getting some help?*
> *OP: Not really.*
> *H: Can you do this all by yourself?*
> *OP: I can do it.*
> *H: You know, he will need daily injections and there will be a number*
> *of necessary personal care tasks. Do you think you're ready to deal with*
> *all of that?*
> *OP: Yes.*

At first glance, the helper's questions seem to communicate care and concerns for the person taking on the care of his partner. But a second look reveals potential hidden messages: You should consider getting help;

you're not able to do this yourself; you might not be ready for the tough stuff. These messages may not be intended by the helper, but they can be construed from the closed questions. If she does have these concerns, it would be better for her to address them through reflection and response and open questions.

Another temptation for the helper following a "yes" or "no" response to a closed question is to ask "why" something is so. From my perspective, this is one of the worst things we can do as helpers. "Why?" tends to provoke defensiveness or shame because it requires us to justify our answers.

H: Were you successful in completing that assignment?
OP: No, I haven't done it yet.
H: Why not?
OP: Because I haven't had time.
H: Why haven't you had the time?
OP: I guess it just wasn't a priority.
H: How come? ["How come...?" is a sneaky way of asking "why?" It usually produces the same kind of defensiveness as a direct "why?"]
OP: I don't know.

The other person could be getting prickly at what he feels are little attacks on his decision not to exercise. Or he could be feeling ashamed of himself for not having followed through.

In this example, what the helper really wants to know is how the other person reached his conclusion, what led him to such a course of action, or what obstacles might be in his way. Her questions don't get her this information. Generally speaking, if a person knows why something is so, he will tell us if we give him time and opportunity to do so. This is especially true when we have not backed him into a corner with closed questions. If he doesn't know why, asking for an explanation will not be productive. Exploring the other person's situation directly through the use of open questions is far more useful, helpful, and rewarding.

Open Questions

An open question is one that cannot be logically answered "yes" or "no." The other person has the freedom to respond in any other way he wishes. He usually further discloses his experience, because he does not feel he has to justify himself. When we ask open questions, we are trying to step into the shoes of the other person to see things the way he does. We are moving into position beside him so we can see and understand what he sees. This is an empathy-building process, rather than a process that provokes defensiveness. Open questions are especially empathic when we combine them with reflection and response:

H: Last week we talked about your getting some exercise. How did you do with the assignment? [open question]

OP: Not very well.

H: What seemed to be the problem? [open question]

OP: I didn't have the time.

H: There wasn't a lot of time, huh? [reflection]

OP: No, with all the other things I had to do, it couldn't be a priority.

H: It sounds like you've got a lot going on right now. It was easy to put the assignment on the back burner. [reflection and response (feedback)]

OP: Yeah, I do. My partner needs a lot of care, and I find I'm really busy doing what I need to do for him. I don't have time to do things for myself.

H: No time for yourself... [reflection]

OP (with a sigh): No.

H: You sound a little sad or discouraged. [reflection (of non-verbal message) or response (feedback)]

OP: I am. I really wish I could do what I need to do to keep myself healthy.

H: You really want the time to take care of yourself. [reflection]

OP: Yeah.

H: So you want to make the time to do the things that are good for you. Walking for 10 minutes a day is one good way to start. What could you do to free up that amount of time for yourself? [response (information giving) and open question]

The helper asks a question, then spends time reflecting the other person's verbal and non-verbal messages and responding with feedback and information. This supports the other person's experience before she asks another question.

Open questions are usually "what?" or "how? questions:

What have you tried to do to fix that problem?
How could you go about solving that problem?
How did you come to that conclusion?
What led you to make that decision?

"When?" and "who?" questions are technically open questions, but they work like closed questions in that they limit the range of possible response to one or two specifics:

H: When are you going to your appointment?
OP: This afternoon.
H: Who is going with you?
OP: My neighbor.

Sometimes we need to know this specific information. At other times, we may want to let the other person explore his own answer, and "what" or "how" is a better way to go:

H: What's your plan for getting to and from your appointment?
OP: I'm planning on going this afternoon. I'll pick my neighbor up on the way. She volunteered to go with me for moral support. Maybe she should even drive in case I can't afterwards. I hadn't thought about that.

The other person tells the helper everything she needs to know as the result of her one open question.

Good Questions

Some questions—open and closed—are useful because they give us needed information. But the best questions are ones that benefit the other person. Questions are helpful because they provide an opportunity for the other person to explore his own thinking. By putting our thoughts into words, spoken or written, we can come to a better understanding of ourselves and our situation, and we can find ways to address our concerns or solve problems.

OP: I'm wondering what to do about my job.

H: What are you wondering? [open question]

OP: Well, there's this feeling I have of being stuck with no prospect of advancement. I'm kind of bored. It feels like there is more I could be doing.

H: So you feel stuck and bored and feel you could be doing something more. [reflection]

OP: Yes, but I don't feel like taking the initiative to reach out in other directions, at least at work.

H: You don't want to put energy into finding new directions at work. What might be directions for you to consider outside of work so far? [reflection and open question]

OP: Well, I'm not really sure at this point.

H: You're not sure, but I'll bet you've done some thinking about it. What are some of the ideas you have come up with? [reflection; response (self-disclosure); open question]

OP: It would be nice to have something I really love to do to invest my time in.

H: You'd like to do what you love, and love what you do. What sort of things to you love to do? [reflection and open question]

OP: I love to garden. I just wish I had enough time for it.

H: Gardening is something you'd like to have time to do. I'm wondering

how you could free up some time to do this, since you love to do it.
[reflection; response (self-disclosure) that suggests a question]

The helper invites the other person to put his wondering about new directions into words with an open question. She then reflects the other person's message and invites further disclosure through another open question. Her question asks the other person to name some of his options for new directions *outside* of work, but he is not sure what they are. So, the helper invites him to talk about some of his thinking at this time, and the other person reveals something important—that loving what he does is important to him.

Using another open question, the helper asks him to name some of the things he loves to do. She reflects his response and continues to help him clarify his thoughts. Her last question in this example is a question that is embedded in her wondering. By sharing the fact that she wonders how he could free up time to do something he loves to do, she invites him to ask himself the same question. At this point, the other person has moved from vague wondering to considering a possible option and ways to make that option possible. The helper's good questions have moved him forward in his thinking.

Embedded Questions

Open and closed questions are "real" questions in the grammatical sense. They begin with what we learned in school are "question words"—what, when, where, how (but not why!)—or with a subject-verb inversion—"you are" becomes "are you." They end with a question mark and a rise in the pitch of our voice. Other methods of inquiry are not really questions, but they act like questions because they encourage the other person to share more information and help him move through his message. These questions are embedded within statements that invite the other person to respond as if he were answering a question:

OP: I know I've been doing a good job this year, but I feel like I'm at

a dead end. I'm considering making some changes.
H: Tell me more about the kinds of changes you are considering.

The helper could have reflected the other person's statement:

H: You are thinking about making some changes in the work you are doing because you feel like you've reached the end of the current road.

Or she could have asked a good question:

H: What kinds of changes are you considering?

Instead, she makes a statement that invites the other person to add to his message.

Statements that invite the other person to "tell me more" carry with them the question *"could you tell me more?"* This implied question is a closed one, however, and the statement avoids the possibility that the other person could reply with a simple "yes" or "no." If the other person does not wish to say more, he can tell us (*"I'd rather not"*), but he is more likely to say a little more that enables us to return to our best interventions, reflection, and response.

Another statement with a hidden question that is useful in helping interactions is the invitation to help us understand:

OP: I really don't like what's going on here. I'm having a real problem accepting this situation and working with it.
H: Help me understand what it is that is of particular concern.

Rather than coming back with reflection, response, or a question, the helper invites the other person to help her see things from his perspective. An embedded question is especially useful when anger is in the equation.

In that case, an open question, such as, *"What's your problem?"* or *"What seems to be the problem?"* might be particularly unhelpful because it could provoke defensiveness. By asking for help in understanding, the helper asks if she might stand in the other person's shoes for a moment. Such a move defuses the situation because the interaction is no longer face-to-face. The helper and the other person are standing side-by-side looking at the problem.

Because these statements with hidden questions are actually commands (grammatically, they are the same as "shut the door" and "bring me my sweater"), we need to be careful of when and how we use them and avoid relying on them as a primary intervention. They work best when nothing else seems right, when we are stuck, or when anger plays a part in the interaction. Like other questions, they should follow reflection and response and be woven into the context of the helping conversation.

Cautions About Questions

Good questions help focus attention of a particular part of an issue or break a big problem into manageable pieces or give a new angle on things. They stimulate different thinking that can produce new ideas, approaches, and viewpoints. They help the other person understand more about his beliefs and values and other concepts that underlie how he thinks about the world.

However, not all good questions are useful or helpful. The *process* of asking questions is as necessary for us to consider as the questions themselves. Asking good questions has risks, and as helpers, we need to be aware of what they are in order to use good questions in a way that is helpful.

Depth

Good questions encourage exploration of the other person's message, and exploration of a message—especially the feelings in or behind it—

can deepen the level of disclosure in a helping encounter. Because our main task is not counseling, helpers need to choose questions that will keep the dialog within the limits of their roles and responsibility. We also must acquire and access an inner sense of when the other person is going into areas we ought not go and know how to return to safe ground.

Generally speaking, questions about content are "safer" than questions about feelings. Exploration of content tends to keep the process in our minds, whereas exploration of feelings shifts to our hearts. If the questions we ask help us stay with the mental process, we are likely to remain at a level of encounter that fits within our scope of practice.

This is not to say that asking and talking about feelings is bad, wrong, or inappropriate. Feelings tend to be "where it's at" in our concerns. Concerns are just concerns. They bother or satisfy us because of the emotions they evoke, and expression of those emotions is sometimes a very necessary component of healing. Emotions exist at different levels within us. Some are close to the surface, while others are hidden. Because of the professional and ethical limits of our work, we are safest staying near the emotional surface. Shallow does not mean superficial or unproductive. Good healing can happen at the tide line and in the quietness of shallow water. We may ask good feeling questions to facilitate the other person's expression of what is there, but we are right not to explore the feelings in depth.

One of our responsibilities as helpers who are not trained as professional counselors is to hold the emotional line. The problem is that feelings emerge in helping encounters as they bubble up within the other person, and we may find ourselves deep in emotional waters through no action of our own beyond asking, "How are you feeling today?" When this happens, we must remember to re-center ourselves so we can be fully present, and return to the skills of reflection and response and content-oriented questions. Doing so provides a "way out" of deep places.

Usually an encounter includes points at which we have the option of choosing the direction, focus, and depth of our interaction.

H: I'm glad to see you today. How are you?
OP: Not too good.
H: Not too good...? [reflection]
OP (eyes filling with tears): My brother is moving to a nursing home

near his kids, and I won't get to see him very often.
H: I see some tears in your eyes, so it seems to me that your brother must be pretty important to you. [feedback; self-disclosure]
OP (beginning to weep): We're twins, so we've been together for 80 years. Even though we're twins I've always been the big brother.

At this point, the helper has a choice of where to go. She can't go right into her primary work as a dietician; too much is in the way for her to be able to find out how the other person is managing his modified diet yet. To be empathic, she needs to help the other person "finish his experience" first.

Finishing an experience does not necessarily mean coming to terms with the whole concern at that time. Rather, we help the other person return to a place of relative stability in which his concern is "zipped up" and tucked away in a place to be explored at a later time. The question for the helper is how best to accomplish this task.

Here are two possible responses:

H (response #1): Eighty years—such a long time! How do you feel about this?
H (response #2): It looks to me like you might be very sad. How are you feeling?

These responses address the other person's feeling in the moment. The first is a good question; the second is self-disclosure, followed by an open question. Since the other person is in his feelings, either of these responses could help him move through and resolve the moment. The good question leaves the field wide open for the other person. He can choose the direction he needs to go.

The second response conveys the helper's perception that the other person feels sad. She checks this out by asking him how he feels. Her response narrows the field before focusing the other person's attention on what he feels. The second response is probably better than the first because it begins with self-disclosure/feedback. The brief shift in focus to the helper interrupts the other person's flow of feelings. Her follow-up question helps him think about and name his experience. Thinking about feelings occurs at a shallower depth than feeling feelings and moves the experience toward completion.

Here are two more possible responses to the other person's disclosure:

H (response #3): This is a big change. How will it feel to live without your brother near by?
H (response #4): This is a big change. What will it be like for you not to have your brother near by?

This set of responses focuses on future time. Responses #3 and #4 address what it will be like for the other person to be separated from his twin brother. Both occur on the level of imagination. The other person can't know what it will be like; he can only imagine. The first of these responses asks him to imagine his possible future feelings. The second response provides an opportunity for a wider variety of response from the other person. He can talk about what he thinks he will feel in the future (*"I think I'll probably be pretty lonely"*). He also could talk about what he won't be able to do with his brother (*"I lose my golf partner, so there goes that"*) or opportunities that the separation could offer (*"Maybe I could stay with my nephew and visit my brother—if they let me travel"*) or any number of other responses.

Emotions happen in the present. Even when we are sad or happy about a past event, we are having those feelings in the present time. When we begin to talk about the past or the future, we are reminiscing and telling stories or imagining and fantasizing (telling a possible story). Reminiscing, telling stories about events or people, imagining, and fantasizing are cognitive processes. They operate out of our heads more than out of our hearts. Good open questions can steer the helping interaction in these directions and better avoid depth of emotion.

Because both responses #3 and #4 ask the other person to think, they will help him shift out of the realm of emotion. By taking the focus away from the present and into the future, the other person is helped out of his current experience into an imaginary one. Both questions have the potential of leading to more feelings, for example, the other person could already feel lonely and shift from experiencing sadness to experiencing loneliness in the present. If that occurs, the helper can reflect and make another response that directs the focus toward thinking, but they are likely to be imagined feelings, rather than here-and-now experienced ones. More likely, the other person will shift out of the feeling place and move into talking about possible situations and circumstances—content areas.

> *H (response #5): Because you two are so close, it seems to me that his moving away will be a big change for you.*
> *H (response #6): Because you two are so close, it seems to me that his moving away will be a big change for both of you.*

These possible responses avoid the use of questions altogether. They are self-disclosure. Moving away or having a close friend or family move away *is* a big change. The helper's responses name that *"big change"* as part of the other person's future experience and are likely to focus his attention on the nature of that change. In response #5, the helper keeps the focus on the other person. She invites him to explore what he imagines the change will bring him. In response #6, she opens the matter up to imagining the changes that will occur for both him and his brother. This response moves the focus away from the other person alone to include someone else. Because, the helper encourages the other person to think beyond himself and move further away from his emotions in the moment, this response is more stabilizing than response #5.

As a general rule, then, good questions that help us avoid deep places are those that return the other person to the realm of thinking and help him focus on matters outside present time and beyond his own concerns. If we feel we are headed into areas beyond the limits of our role and responsibility, these provide ways back to safe ground. They serve us well as ways of helping the other person "finish the experience" so that we can move on to our other work together.

Interrogating

Like other responses, good questions are most effective if interwoven with reflection. Too many questions, especially if they are asked quickly one after the other, can sound and feel like an interrogation or interview. Reflection follows up a question with empathy and enables us to express interest in what the other person has said before moving on to the next topic.

Look at the differences in these two examples:

OP: I'm a bit worried about the cost of all this.
H: What is it about the cost that worries you?
OP: I'm afraid I'll be too much in debt.
H: What would it be like to be more in debt than you are now?
OP: I'm not sure I'll be able to pay the bills.
H: What could you do to manage this situation?
OP: I don't know that I can.
H: Who might be able to help you?

In this encounter, the helper asks question after question without pausing to reflect on and consider what the other person has said. The other person might feel pushed against the wall and not heard or understood. Or he might have concerns that are more important to him than thinking about who could help him. He might want and need to say more along the way.

OP: I'm a bit worried about the cost of all this.
H: What is it about the cost that worries you?
OP: I'm afraid I'll be too much in debt.
H: You're afraid of more debt. [reflection]
OP: Yeah. I've just managed to get myself on steady financial ground and I just can't go back to the place where I'm not sure I'll be able to pay the bills. I'm worried that might happen.
H: You're worried. It would be hard to go back to that place, especially

after having worked so hard to get out of it. [reflection]

OP: Yeah.

H: How do you think you might manage this situation? [good question]

OP: I don't know that I can do it by myself. All I seem to know is how to get into debt. I needed help getting out last time. Now, maybe I need some help staying out of debt.

H: You've had help in the past and it sounds to me like you're thinking that getting some help again might be a good idea. Who might be able to help you with this current situation so that you don't have to worry so much? [reflection; self-disclosure; good question]

In this encounter, the helper uses reflection, response, and good questions to help the other person explore his situation. He feels heard, understood, and supported in his concern and finds his own possible solution.

Prodding v. Probing

Our goal is to establish the empathic connection in which we can do our primary work. The purpose of our asking questions is to help the other person express himself, not to pry into his concerns. Questions are tools for opening opportunities for that expression, and asking questions is a process of gently probing a concern to encourage the other person to express the thoughts and feelings he is having.

To use good questions well, we must be interested in what the other person is experiencing. The quality of our presence and attention communicate our curiosity and interest more than anything else. Once we learn to ask questions, we have a tendency to forget about our own centeredness and focus on drawing out the other person's story. Our empathy becomes nosiness, and our gently probing becomes prodding. One of my own experiences provides a metaphor for this difference:

I recall one New England winter that seemed to go on forever. To satisfy my longing for spring, I forced some narcissus bulbs. I tucked them into some marble chips root end down, gave them plenty of water, put them in some sunlight, and waited. And waited. And watched. I could see the green tips of leaves peeping up in the papery skin of the bulbs, but they seemed to be taking a very long time to grow. Eventually, I became concerned that perhaps something was wrong with the bulbs, so I pried up the edge of one of them to check on the roots. The roots looked like good roots, so I tucked the bulb back in the chips and waited and watched some more.

I complained to my sister about my slow growing bulbs when she came to visit. She took a look at them, stuck her finger in the gravel, and suggested I give them water. The roots needed to stay wet. With fresh water over the course of the next week, most of the bulbs took off and grew like crazy as if they had just been waiting for the right support for their growth. The bulb that didn't was the one I had poked and prodded.

The point of this story is not to highlight my early struggle as a gardener but to illustrate the difference between prodding and probing. I had prodded. In my impatience to make things happen, I handled the first bulb roughly, suspecting there was something wrong with it. My sister, on the other hand, had probed. She'd looked carefully at the bulbs, explored their environment, and noticed they needed my attention and some nourishment. The bulbs that were probed grew; the one that was prodded did not.

When we act out of curiosity to make something happen in healing interactions, we are distracted from being present and allowing what is present for the other person to be there and unfold on its own terms. We ask questions, hoping to uncover the problem. We prod the other person to move according to our timetable and in our direction, rather than his. When we act out of interest in helping the other person express himself, we can ask questions that enable him to tell us what is happening. We probe gently around the center of his concern to see what he needs to move forward in his process.

Doing Something

At times helpers feel the need to "do something." Questions are an easy way to meet this need, but they are often not particularly helpful. Compared to reflection and response, questions are tools that enable us to be most active in our helping encounters. But that's a problem, and one reason why asking questions is one of the least helpful interactions. It seems to be that the more active we are, the less present we tend to be. Perhaps this is because the process of forming and asking good questions puts us more in ourselves than in the other person's place. We do need to include ourselves in our awareness of what is happening in our helping encounters, but the other person must stand at the center of our inclusive vision.

If we feel the need to "do something," we may be drifting into "fixing." When we witness someone's experience, especially if the other person is struggling with a serious matter or in emotional pain, we may be tempted to ease the burden or relieve the pain. Staying with intense emotions is difficult to do. We'd rather things change and be "all better," so that the other person is relieved from suffering and we are spared from witnessing it.

Because questions take people out of emotions and into the mind, they serve as means for changing the emotional tone of an interaction. That is why they work to help us steer away from depth at choice points in the middle of an encounter. But what if the other person already is into his emotions when we first encounter him? This occurred to me on an occasion as I walked into the room with my harp. I hadn't done or said anything. I just happened to be there, and he started to cry.

Feelings are natural; they happen when they need to happen. When the dam breaks, emotions rush out, and then they usually subside. The best thing we can do for the other person if this happens is to be there in supportive silence, hand him a tissue, touch his hand, if that feels right, and wait. It can be a challenge to stay in the company of strong emotion, particularly grief, but it can make a profound difference for the person experiencing that emotion to know support is near. We do not need to do anything to fix the situation or make the other person feel better.

Until the other person can talk about what he is feeling, we should take advantage of the opportunity to be silent, instead of reflecting, responding, or asking questions. When his feelings subside, we can offer the opportunity to talk or address our reason for being there. In my case, the other person stopped crying and asked for some music. Should the other person's emotions not subside or they get worse, or the person becomes agitated, it's time for us to call in help from others.

Another time at which we can experience the need to do something occurs when we wish to avoid our own experience. When we are truly present with another person as a witness to his experience, we are likely to have an emotional response. Because of the universal nature of core experiences, we probably have had occasion to feel what another person feels even though our circumstances may have been different.

We can be tempted to run from our reaction and move the other person away from his own experience so that we don't have to feel what we feel by asking a question to hide behind. The problem is that we would not be asking that question to serve the other person. We would be serving ourselves. The question would not be based in empathy; it would be grounded in our desire to get away from our own pain.

Running or hiding from an experience can make matters worse. When we try to push something away, we actually push it into the front of our awareness where it takes up space in a way that keeps us from being present with what is happening in the moment. While we are hiding from our reaction or trying not to feel a certain way, we expend energy on ourselves and move away from being with the other person.

When we have an emotional response prompted by the other person's disclosure, whether as a result of witnessing his experience or remembering our own, asking a question is not the way out. Asking a question may relieve briefly our immediate emotional response and return the focus to the other person, but it costs us our centeredness and ability to be present. We are still left with what is happening inside of us.

Our best course of action is to practice genuineness and admit—at least to ourselves—that we are having feelings, too. Being genuine does not necessarily mean expressing our feelings; it means acknowledging them. Naming feelings acknowledges they are there. Once we have acknowledged them, they no longer beg for attention. The feelings may still be there, but they are likely to remain in the background and out of our way as we work with the other person. Once we have completed the interaction, we can find a time, place, and healthy way to take care of ourselves. For example:

> *OP: I can't believe she wants a divorce. I feel so hurt and angry—and really upset that we can't work things out.*
>
> *H (response #1): How will you manage?*
>
> *H (response #2): I was so angry when my husband left me. It makes me upset all over again when I hear what's happened to you. How dare people do this to other people?*
>
> *H (response #3): Right now, I feel sad, too. I think it is very hard when important relationships can't heal.*

The helper recalls her own experience of divorce and re-experiences her hurt and anger and feels sad about not having been able to keep her marriage intact.

The first response is an example of a helper's attempt to avoid her own experience. She asks a question that is not particularly important, nor does it reflect what the other person has said. In the second response, the helper expresses her own feelings in the way she is feeling them—angry and sad—and diverts the interaction away from both her and the other person into a discussion about how people can do this sort of thing. In both these situations, the helper is compromised by her own feelings and appears distracted and disinterested in the other person. The third helper acknowledges that she feels sad. She doesn't talk about her own experience other than to relate her thought that breakups of significant relationships are difficult. Because she names her feelings, they can find a place to rest so that she can be comfortably present with the other person.

Summary

Asking questions can be the best course of action at times. A well-timed question can nudge the conversation and keep it going. A gentle probe can stimulate further disclosure. A good question can open the door to new ideas and new ways of looking at a situation, and help us focus and direct the interaction toward healing and away from areas we ought not to explore.

Sometimes questions aren't the most helpful response we can make in a healing encounter. Something shifts once we give ourselves permission to ask questions. We more easily forget about listening, reflection, and response and drift off center. Asking questions seems easier than doing something else.

Reflection and response require careful attention to what the other person is saying and experiencing. We don't have to listen as carefully when we know we can ask questions and catch up on what we haven't heard. Our task as helpers is to learn to use questions effectively as we foster the empathic connection and move toward cooperative work.

CHAPTER 7
THE HEART OF THE MATTER

Centering, listening, reflecting, responding, and asking questions—these skills form the core of the process of helping. When we look at these skills in isolation as we did, we dissect the process of helping interaction, rather than seeing it as a whole. This is rather like dissecting a body organ. It's useful and important to know the structure of the heart and how it works. Knowing how the heart functions as part of the whole body, how it interacts and works with other organs, is even more useful. In that light, we see that the heart and the other body organs contribute to a whole that is much greater than the sum of its parts.

In earlier chapters, we explored the anatomy of the helping interaction. In this chapter, we will explore the process of putting them together into a system of helping interaction. We also will consider some guidelines for ethical practice as helpers, and we'll close with a discussion of some of the beneficial side effects of helping.

Seeing the Big Picture

Since every helping encounter is different, generating a formula for how to put the skills together in the "right" way is impossible. A "one-size-fits-all" guide to how to do it "right" will never exist.

The potential for healing exists within the encounter and emerges from our presence in the relationship. Helping interaction accesses and activates that potential with a blend of the skills that meets the other person's needs for self-expression and clears the way to the work we are doing together. Letting go of thinking in terms of finding the *right* way and framing the process in terms of finding an *effective* way to work within each encounter is more helpful to us as caregivers.

Some of those with whom we work will need only our presence and reflection to move through a concern. Others may want information. Still others may benefit from an invitation to say more. Sometimes we need to be quiet and let things unfold and resolve on their own. At other times, we need to be more active in focusing and directing the interaction.

Learning new skills requires us to practice and put our knowledge to work in a conscious, deliberate way and to develop the confidence that lets us rely on our understanding and ability. When we have this confidence, we are free to focus on thinking about and sensing what intervention will be more effective. In time, considering the most effective intervention becomes less deliberate and develops into a more unconscious, natural flow of action that best fits the situation. Our new knowledge gets fully absorbed into what we already know. If we stop at intellectually understanding the skills and do not cultivate our ability to use them, we short-circuit the value of learning. We need to put knowledge into action to reap the benefit of understanding.

Putting the pieces together coherently and effectively is a matter of practice. *Practice*—the word can conjure up images of experimenting and guinea pigs. What right to we have to make the people with whom we are working guinea pigs and experiment on them? My answer to that question is "none."

Another way of construing practice is used in law, medicine, and counseling, and in disciplines such as meditation or yoga. In this sense, practice reminds us we are engaged in a process of helping others in which we learn skills, apply knowledge a step at a time, and build the ability to rely on our knowledge and skill with confidence, knowing we can always learn more.

If we approach our practice of helping skills as the *exercise* of what we are learning, rather than as *experimentation*, we move from the idea of testing and proving a skill to strengthening our understanding and learning with every encounter. In this conceptualization objectivity shifts to subjectivity. We aren't observing our skills in a vacuum; we are experiencing them from within a relationship. We aren't applying our skills to the outside of our work; we are living them from the inside out.

The people with whom we work aren't guinea pigs; they are partners in the learning process. If we bring healthy attitudes to our practice, we can participate in this partnership in ways that are responsible, professional, and ethical.

Thinking About Ethics

Nurses and lawyers and many other professionals who are engaged in working with others have clearly defined codes of practice. These codes help professionals conduct themselves in ways that keep the interest of the people they are helping at the priority. Members of professions with a code of ethics are required to subscribe to the standards of behavior and the principles described in the code, using them as guidelines for their decisions and actions in their work with others. The ethical aspect of the professionals' interaction with others is evaluated according to these standards. If a professional acts contrary to these standards, she can forfeit her right to practice.

Guidelines for what constitutes ethical practice are written in a profession-specific way that addresses the unique requirements, roles, and challenges that emerge in the particular work of the members of that profession. For example, psychiatrists, psychologists, and mental health counselors provide counseling, but each profession has its own code of ethics, due to important differences in the work of members of these professions.

Consequently, writing an ethical code that applies to everyone who is the position of helping others is not possible. Given helpers varying roles and the different circumstances of our work, such a code also would not be desirable. However, all helpers—professionals and volunteers—should cultivate a way of thinking about the challenges they may face and develop a personal understanding of what it means to be an ethical practitioner in the kinds of helping relationships they have.

To a large extent, the study of professional ethics is not learning what the most ethical course of action is. Rather, we learn how to think about the factors involved in an ethical decision and how to arrive at a decision about the most ethical course of action. We will encounter situations as helpers in which we need to make difficult decisions about what to do. We may find we have options that will seem equally unfavorable.

In some cases, courses of action will be clear, because we must, should, and ought to do some things to be helpers who do no harm. In other cases, we will need to wrestle with our options to determine what is best for the other person. We need to have an understanding of the kinds of things to consider in making ethical decisions *before* we find ourselves in a dilemma.

We can start thinking about what is ethical by looking at some of the broad areas of concern that are usually covered in ethical codes of professional helpers. The guidelines for decision making with regard to these concerns were put into the code because years of experience show that they lead to actions that best protect the welfare of the person being helped. If we keep these in mind, with our personal beliefs about what is ethical, we are far more likely to act with others in ways that are ethical in helping interactions.

Hippocrates's Lesson

In ancient Greece, the physician and teacher Hippocrates enjoined healers to cultivate two habits: to help and to do no harm. This is the bottom line in ethical practice for all helpers. All decisions we make and actions we take in helping interactions should be directed to helping the other person meet his own needs and further his own purpose.

We need to suspend any desire we have to fix things or to impose solutions that come from our own agenda or belief system. We must consider who will benefit from what we intend to say or do and the range of likely consequences of our choices. By getting ourselves out of the way, we have a far better chance of being helpful and, at the very least, not causing harm. If we can't get ourselves out of the way mentally and emotionally, our most ethical course of action is to refrain from trying to help until we see our way clear to attending to the other person's welfare.

Personal Ethics

To be ethical practitioners, we must have a clear sense of what is important to us. Professional codes of ethics describe what the values of a profession are, but as helpers, we bring to our work personal values as well. If we do not have a professional code of ethics as a guideline for ethical decision-making, we must operate on our own values. In either case, our personal values will influence our thinking about what is ethical, and knowing what our values are helps us make hard decisions from steady ground.

Here's an example:

Mariana was an intern in a state welfare office. Part of her responsibility was to organize incoming applications for welfare benefits for her supervisor to review. There was a back-up in the case load, and applications were organized by date and reviewed in chronological order. As she was sorting through the cases, she came across an application submitted by one of her neighbors. She knew this family was badly in need of benefits, and they had asked her to keep an eye out for the file and "do what she could" to move things along.

Mariana knew she could help them by placing the file close to the top of the stack. She knew that no one would know whether she slipped it in ahead of the others or not, and she suspected that other workers in her office did that sort of thing.

Mariana could help her friends, but that would mean bumping some other needy family down the list. If she chose to put her friends' file where it belonged—behind everyone else's—they would have to wait for a long time before they received benefits they needed and deserved. It seemed to her that either way, one person benefited at the expense of another. Furthermore, if she put the file in order and the family asked about it, Mariana would either have to lie to them or tell them she had not done as they wished. Before she took action, she decided to talk to me—her internship mentor—about her dilemma.

There was no professional code of ethics to guide Mariana's decision making, so she had to consider what the right thing to do would be. She was in a position to help friends, and she believed that helping her neighbors was important. She could rationalize a decision to put the file near the top by saying that it really wasn't all that big a deal—it was only one family; it wouldn't hold up everyone else for very long. Besides, everyone in the office did that sort of thing. No one would know.

But Mariana also believed that honesty was important. As we talked about the case, she realized that honesty was one of her personal values, that it did not matter whether anyone else knew she was being honest or not. She would know, and she valued knowing that she was an honest person more than she valued helping her friends. She considered honesty important enough to tell her friends she had put their file in the proper order, if they asked. Mariana decided that the most ethical thing for her to do was to use her personal value, honesty, as the ground for making her decision. She was able to do this because she had explored her values.

Consultation

Mariana did not just make her decision herself. She talked to me about her concerns, and was able to decide what was best based on our conversation about her personal values, her position as a helper, the implications about her possible choices, and what the most ethical course of action would be. Rather than acting quickly, she thought about what was important to her and consulted another helping professional.

Even the most experienced helpers encounter situations in which they do not know what the most ethical course of action is in a helping interaction. When that occurs we need to ask for help from colleagues and supervisors who can cast a more objective look at the situation, bring a fresh perspective, and help us sort through questions and concerns.

Seeking supervision, inviting collaboration, and consulting with others are endeavors that help us stay honest. The data from studies of patterns of ethical complaints about helping professionals show that those who get into ethical difficulty are those who practice in isolation. Those who ask questions of each other and invite colleagues and supervisors to witness their work tend to avoid compromising the ethics of their practice. We can't know all the answers. That does not mean we need to stop helping, but it does point to our need to seek input from others when we are in doubt as to what to do.

All helpers need someone they can go to for consultation. If we work or volunteer in an organization, we usually have a supervisor we can talk to when we need help. If we work in a private practice, we should have a network of colleagues to serve as a sounding board for our concerns. Whenever we are in doubt about the right thing to do in a helping relationship, we should consult with a supervisor or with others whose integrity and knowledge we respect.

Competency

As ethical helpers we should be well trained in our work and fully function within the scope of our role and responsibility. We must be qualified to do what we do and cultivate our competency through self-directed study and continuing education. We do not venture into practice in areas that are new to us without additional training and supervision. Here's an example from my own experience:

I undertook my internship as a therapeutic harp practitioner in a hospital intensive care unit. I was in close contact with both the nurses on the unit and my internship supervisor. I asked questions and learned how to play healing music for patients in that setting.
Following my internship, I continued to help in ICU, and I volunteered to play for residents in the hospice house near the hospital. At that point, I had solid experience playing therapeutic music for people who were critically ill, but I had never played for anyone who was dying. Helping in the hospice was new work for me. I spent a good deal of time getting to know the other staff members, asking lots of questions, and observing them interacting with patients. I read books and listened to continuing education tapes on death, dying, grief, and bereavement. It was only then that I felt competent to play for someone whose death was immanent.

Ensuring that we remain competent as helpers means taking advantage of opportunities for continuing education. Many worksites offer professional development seminars on site. Many professional organizations sponsor workshops outside of the workplace. Competent helpers participate in training that keeps their knowledge and skills up-to-date.

Self-Care

Ethical practice is grounded in the condition of the helper. Unless we are in good condition, mentally, emotionally, physically, and spiritually, we cannot help in a way that does not potentially jeopardize the wellbeing of the person with whom we are working. We must know, heal, and help ourselves before we can do the same for others. As ethical helpers we know who we are, and we attend to our broken places and weak spots.

This does not mean we are perfect—or even striving to be perfect. It does mean we have a relationship with ourselves that enables us to be aware of where, when, and how we are imperfect and to take steps to make progress toward being the best person we can be. We notice when we are emotionally hooked into unsound patterns of interaction that can harm us and the person we are helping.

Ethical helpers recognize that their own problems can impair their ability to care for others. To be ethical helpers, we must be able to assess honestly our capacity for helping others at a given point in our lives. We cannot be present when our own issues, emotional responses, or personal circumstances weigh heavily on our minds and hearts. If we cannot fully engage in the helping process, we should refrain from trying so that we can take care of ourselves and not cause harm to others.

A Helping Attitude

Because we are working with people, our fundamental attitude about the nature of people is an important factor in our ability to make decisions that do no harm. Before we can act ethically, we must hold the universal worth of every person in high regard, see people as good and valuable, and tolerate their infinite diversity. We may not like or respect a particular person, but we must afford him the right to be who he is.

There may be times when we encounter someone to whom we cannot bring an attitude of positive regard. We cannot help someone we find disgusting, repulsive, or evil or whose personality or lifestyle is so contrary to our own understanding of what is good and right that we find it impossible to meet him with acceptance. We do not need to like all the people we are asked to help, but we must accept who they are and be able to bring empathy, genuineness, and positive regard into our work with them. If we can not, the most ethical course of action is to refrain from engaging with them as a helper.

Physical Intimacy and Touch

Helping interaction brings two people into a relationship with each other. Every healthy relationship includes a boundary—the point at which one person ends and the other person begins. Different kinds of relationships have different expectations of what those boundaries should be.

Maintaining a healthy boundary in helping interactions is particularly important—and particularly challenging—because helping relationships can include moments of emotional intensity, even in the most ordinary situations. When we are truly present with another person and seek understanding, we engage with him at a level not usually experienced in most everyday relationships. Furthermore, when we join with others around sensitive concerns, strong emotions, and major life circumstances and transitions, we meet at the heart of what really matters. This is an exquisite moment, one of tenderness, understanding, and compassion.

Meeting at the heart of the matter makes helping work. It also offers one of the greatest risks of helping interaction—the temptation to convert the experience into sexual intimacy. If a helper gives in to this temptation, she is no longer a helper in the relationship. The helping relationship ends because the helper and the other person are now involved in a different way.

As helpers—volunteer or professional—whose work is not held to a formal code of ethics, we are in the position of having to determine for ourselves what the boundary between us and those we help should be when it comes to physical intimacy. Our principle guideline is the welfare of the other person. Since sexual intimacy dissolves the helping relationship and usually results in harm to the person being helped, the welfare of the other person rests on the decision not to engage in such intimacy if the helping relationship came first. If we are in a sexually intimate relationship with someone who asks for our assistance as a helper, we must consider carefully the issues involved before creating a helping relationship with him.

The issue of non-sexual touch in helping relationships is a topic of considerable ethical debate among helping professionals. The meaning of touch can be easily misunderstood, and even casual physical contact can cross the boundary between helpers and those with whom they work. Because of the special nature of their helping relationships, professional counselors and psychotherapists are advised to be very guarded when it comes to touching their clients. As helpers who are not trained counselors, we may not have the same ethical constraint and must make our own decisions about whom, how and when we touch in our work.

Our role as helpers may focus on touching others. The work of helpers such as massage therapists, Reiki practitioners, and nurses, for example, calls for physical contact between the helper and person being helped. Other helpers such as therapeutic music practitioners, social service caseworkers, and lawyers routinely do not touch the people with whom they are working. If our primary work does not involve physical contact and we wish to touch a person we are helping, we need to be sure that doing so is appropriate for our professional purpose, setting, and circumstances and in the best interest of the other person, and that the meaning of our touch is clearly one of care, not intimacy.

Touch can be a gesture of support, an invitation to sexual intimacy, or an act of abuse. Some people are fortunate enough to know only the caring side of touch; others have learned from experience that physical contact is something to be avoided. A touch of the hand, pat on the arm, or hug can communicate empathy, support, and comfort. On the other hand, these gestures can be misconstrued as an invitation to sexual involvement, experienced as threatening or patronizing, or considered too personal or intrusive.

Comfort with touch is, in part, culturally and socially determined. For example, in the Euro-American subculture of the northeastern United States, people tend to be very conservative with regard to touching those they do not know well. In other regions of the country and in cultures and subcultures across the world, the social norms regarding physical contact are different.

Because people vary in the extent to which they are comfortable with touch, those of us who are helpers need to think carefully about how "touchy" we are in our helping interaction. We should remain well within our own comfort zone with regard to touch, and remember that others' comfort zone may be very different from ours. We are better off erring on the side of reserve than using touch in a manner that might offend the other person or create misunderstanding. If the person we are helping withdraws from our touch, we should refrain from touching him again. The same is true if the person with whom we are working over-responds to our touch in a way that is inappropriate to the situation or that makes us feel uncomfortable.

Using touch as a nonverbal accompaniment to a verbal message (rather than using touch alone to express our support) is one way to avoid miscommunication. For example, a homecare volunteer might verbally greet the person she is visiting as she touches his hand. A social services worker might reassure the adolescent she is helping with words and a hand on the shoulder. In this way, these helpers link their touch with a verbal message that makes it clear that the intent of their physical contact is empathy, not intimacy.

As helpers, we should restrict supportive touch to parts of the body that are "neutral," usually the hand, arm, shoulder, upper back, knee, and top of the foot. Generally speaking, the face, head, neck, torso, and upper leg are more personal areas of the body. We should consider our role and circumstances before touching others there. For example, a supervisor probably would not have justifiable cause to stroke an employee's forehead. But this kind of touch might be very kind and healing when done by a hospice volunteer for someone who is actively dying.

Hugs are "iffy" matters because of their potential for intimacy, but they are not always inappropriate. I choose not to initiate hugs with those with whom I am working. If the other person does so, I can stop and decide whether I want to join the hug or offer a handshake or touch on the arm instead. For me, putting an arm around someone's shoulder is an option that communicates the support and empathy of a hug and guards against misunderstanding. Shaking hands is almost always considered appropriate in Western culture. "Two-handed handshakes" in which we grip the back of the other person's hand with our left hand while shaking right hands are often good, warm, alternatives to hugs.

Overlapping Relationships

As helpers, we need to be aware of the implications of having more than one kind of relationship with someone we are helping. We overlap relationships with someone when we are his helper and a friend, neighbor, colleague, member of his family, etc. With overlapping relationships comes the risk of a conflict of interest in which what we need to do in one role is contrary to what we need to do in the other.

Many professionals are ethically prohibited from treating their friends and family members. For example, a surgeon would be advised not to operate on her partner; a counselor should not enter into a psychotherapeutic relationship with a friend. Other professional codes of ethics also caution helpers to avoid establishing non-sexual overlapping relationships with those they are helping. Again, helpers who are members of these professions must make decisions about overlapping relationships according to these guidelines.

A host of other helpers do routinely "treat" family members, and friends. A massage therapist might give her partner a massage. A therapeutic music practitioner is likely to play for an ailing friend. A Reiki practitioner may find herself on the same committee with someone she treats. A yoga teacher and a student in her class discover a mutual interest and become friends.

Because of the intensity of the connections and disconnections we form with others, the bonds we form with a person in one relationship can enhance or weaken those we have with the same person in another relationship. This works as long as the overlapping relationships are mutually enhancing. But when they fail to be so, harm tends to happen to one of the relationships. To be an ethical helper, you need to consider the potential implications of having overlapping relationships.

One way to think about the wisdom of overlapping a helping relationship and a non-helping relationship is to consider which relationship is more important to *both* you and the other person. If one of the relationships were to succeed at the expense of the other, which would you both want that to be? Will adding a second relationship to the first relationship jeopardize the one you both most want to keep? How will the non-helping relationship support or interfere with your ability to work together in the helping relationship?

Considering the answers to questions like these can guide you to making an ethical decision. If your non-helping relationship will jeopardize the welfare of the other person in your helping relationship, one of the relationships should go.

Codependency

Self-help bookshelves are full of books about codependency, a dysfunctional way of being with others in which one person meets her needs by over-investing in the problems of another. Because she needs the other person to need her help, she acts in a way that keeps the other person's problem alive. In other words, she is dependent on the other person's dependency on her. If she were truly helpful, the other person might solve his problem—but then she would be out of a job and have to meet her needs herself.

Helping others is satisfying work. It's no shame to admit that. To a certain extent, we are engaged in working with others because we get something out of it. We put time and attention into others and invest in their care. It feels good to know we are making a difference and that our helping presence matters to someone, but our investment in someone's wellbeing can become harmful—or at least unhelpful. Learning to recognize the point at which we risk becoming codependent is part of the process of maintaining good boundaries and effectiveness as a helper.

Here is a case to explore as an example of codependency:

Benni is an aide in a rehabilitation center for amputees. She enjoys working with the patients because they are so challenged in their ability to do things. She is particularly invested in caring for Mr. Jones who reminds her of her father, a paraplegic. She spends much of her with him encouraging him to talk about his experience in Vietnam and the difficulty he has had managing his life since his wife died.

Benni is often overheard saying things like "Let me do that," "Here, I'll take care of that," and "I'll sort it out for you." She stays late often to take care of Mr. Jones at the evening meal and hovers like a mother hen before leaving for the day. Sometimes on her days off, she will call the unit see how things are going or drop in when she is "just passing by."

Mr. Jones has come to rely on her constant help, and he is cranky with the rest of the staff because he thinks they do not take care of him as well as Benni does. His occupational therapist is considerably challenged by his lack of progress in learning how to do things for himself.

Benni wants to help, and she considers her interest in and care of Mr. Jones to be helping him. But what is the focus of her attention and whom is she really helping? The relationship she has with Mr. Jones is a strong one, but not a helpful one. Benni is over-invested as a helper and is satisfying *her* need to be helpful rather than helping Mr. Jones meet his. She has kept Mr. Jones dependent on her—and depended on his dependency. If he were to learn to do things for himself, he would be discharged. Benni would feel the loss of the relationship profoundly because his problems have provided a way for her to avoid having to take care of herself in healthy ways.

Our efforts to help become unhelpful when *caring* becomes *carrying*. Care in a helping relationship is present when we are actively engaged in the helping process. The other person should occupy our complete attention when we are with him. If we are working with someone over time, care lies dormant between encounters and resurfaces through our complete attention when we meet in the next helping session. It fades when our help is no longer needed.

Carrying occurs when we find our attention focused on the other person when we are not actively engaged in helping him. When we are carrying another person, we do more than just think occasionally about the person with whom we are working. We are preoccupied with the desire to attend to his needs outside of our designated time together and neglect our other responsibilities. His problems take up room in our head, and we find ourselves drawn more and more into the relationship and away from building and maintaining healthy relationships outside of work.

Preoccupation with the concerns of the person we are helping is one of the best clues that we are shifting from caring to carrying. We can recognize preoccupation through a felt sense. We feel it in our bodies as a physical draw to the other person's care or through an awareness of distracted thinking. Our minds think more about the other person than what we are doing in the present moment.

Codependency is sneaky. We can cross the line between caring and carrying without knowing it until we discover that we are too invested in this particular helping relationship. Because we are caught up in the helping relationship, we don't see the codependent dynamic unfolding, and it often takes a friend, family member, or coworker to point out to us what is happening.

I had an occasion to hear of an experience of a therapeutic music practitioner who played for hospice patients. Here's what she told me about what she felt, thought, and did that day:

When I arrived, the spiritual care counselor introduced me to M. whose wife was dying. M. and his wife were in their mid-thirties. They had hoped to have kids, but when they sought help after repeated attempts to conceive, they discovered she had uterine cancer. Their efforts to treat the cancer failed, and her decline had come very quickly.

M. asked me if I would play at his wife's bed side. His wife was unconscious, but seemed relaxed and pain-free. M. talked a good deal about how much he was going to miss his wife. He held her hand and stroked her face as I played. I found myself really wanting to stay, and I played for them for about two hours.

When it came time for me to leave, I was reluctant to go. I had hoped I could be there when M.'s wife died to accompany her transition and support M. But she lingered, and I had to go. I said good-by to M. and his wife and wished her well on her journey. As I left the room, M. crawled up on the bed to lie down beside his wife and hold her in his arms. I began to weep at the sight of his manifest love for his wife and the significance of the loss he faced.

I carried my experience of M. and his wife with me as I played for other residents. I don't think I did a very good job attuning to them and providing the most beneficial music.

Before I left for the day, I felt a strong urge to return to M. and his wife. I stopped in the middle of the hall, suddenly aware of how invested I was in their situation. Maybe it was M.'s love, the fact that they were so young, or that it might have been me in his wife's position. Whatever, I was "hooked."

I had a choice: I could respond to the "hook" by checking on them, or I could go home. Was my desire to see them again compassionate or selfish? I stood there for quite a while trying to decide what was best. The spiritual care counselor saw me standing in the hallway and drew me aside to talk the matter out. She helped me see that I had played a lovely flow of music, been there for M. and his wife, and given them my attention and care. I had said a heartfelt good-bye to them.

Returning to the room was likely to reopen an experience that had had a time of its own and a natural conclusion. I was not likely to be more helpful than I had already been. I had done what I was there to do, and other staff members were just as caring as I was.

I was exceptionally moved by this case. It triggered something in me. I think that I was flooded by a lot of grief when I was with them. I'm not yet sure what I am grieving, but I felt it. I could avoid my grief by focusing on M. and his feelings. When I left that room, however, my sad feelings came back.

My desire to return to their presence had a lot to do with being able to hide behind M's experience again rather than feel what I was feeling. Going back to see them would have been more about me than M. and his wife. I went home instead.

I learned when I came in the next week that M's wife had died the morning after I had been there. M. had conveyed to the staff his appreciation of the music. He said it had helped him grieve, and he knew that it had helped his wife. He was particularly grateful that I had simply left him to hold her and the memory of the music.

I was so glad that the spiritual care counselor had helped me recognize my over-investment in this case and that I had been able to let go of it, rather than satisfying my desire to continue the connection in a codependent way. I now know that going back to see them would not have been helpful. I would have interrupted a profound experience to meet my own needs. Letting go of M. and his wife was the best thing I could have done for them, even though it was the hardest thing for me. I had to do my own crying.

With the help of her coworker, this practitioner recognized she was crossing the line between caring and carrying. She had had a meaningful encounter that affected her in a way that other helping moments had not. Her preoccupation with caring for M. and his wife interrupted her work with others, and she was sorely tempted to satisfy her own need to be with them. She took time instead to explore the meaning behind the impulse to return and recognized that it was easier to ease the husband's grief than face her own.

She saw that she had narrowed her focus to include only this couple and herself, forgetting that she was not the only compassionate helper at the hospice house. To the contrary, she may have lacked compassion in her presence with other residents because of her preoccupation with M. Her work with this couple was done, and it was time for her to let go, take care of herself in other ways, and let others continue to care for M. and his wife.

Confidentiality

Confidentiality is an ethical and legal issue. Numerous laws protect people seeking medical care. Helpers working in a health-care setting are required to know and abide by these laws. For example, many states require helpers to report cases of suspected child or elder abuse to a designated state agency. Laws also describe who has the right *not* to disclose anything about the people with whom they work, even when subpoenaed by a court, usually limited to lawyers and clergy, and who *must* disclose information in legal cases.

Beyond the legal aspects of confidentiality are ethical considerations. Other people are willing to let us help them because they trust us to protect their best interests. One of the ways in which we keep the trust of those we help is by working in a "confidentiality-conscious" way. That means we understand what confidentiality is in the kind of helping relationships we have. It also means that we know where the line is between ethical and unethical disclosure of information about the other person with regard to what we say, when we say it, and to whom we say it.

Confidentiality can be one of the easier ethical determinations to make, in part because of the laws surrounding the issue and in part because most of us like the right to privacy. We understand what it means to protect the privacy of someone else. Counselors, psychotherapists, physicians, lawyers, and other trained helpers know that ethical confidentiality is well described in their professional codes of ethics. Helpers who are not trained counselors do not have the benefit of formal ethical guidelines to follow.

When helpers err in matters of confidentiality, they either say too much or say too little. Keeping information confidential does not mean keeping secrets when doing so would potentially harm the person we are helping or withholding information that could be important to his care. It means that we protect the identity of the person we are helping and that we share information about that person only with those who have a need and right to know.

Occasions arise when we need to be able to talk about the people with whom we are working. One example is a meeting with a person who is overseeing our work, such as a supervisor or clinical director. Another is a treatment team of helpers working with the same person. A third is when we have questions about someone's care and we need to ask for help.

When we need to reveal information about the people with whom we are working, we must be sure that we are choosing the right person to talk to and the right time and place to talk. I notice when I am talking to my supervisor at the hospital, she closes the door if we discuss patients. We don't talk about patients in the elevator or walking down the hall. These are private conversations. I do talk to her about my work, though, including the names of patients and details about them, because I often need her assistance in solving a problem or other support. In terms of the meaning of the word "confidentiality," I am not keeping my work a secret, but I am acting within the limits of the ethic of confidentiality.

As ethical helpers, we should never disclose the identity of the people with whom we are working with anyone outside of the circle of helpers who are also involved with that person and our work with him. On occasion, helpers may be invited to "share a case" with colleagues for educational purposes. In those situations, we must disguise any information that could potentially identify the person whose case we are discussing. In writing this book, for example, I have used some real cases, but I have changed names, gender, ages, and some of their circumstances in a way that protects the identity of the people I am talking about.

Beneficial Side Effects of Helping

One of the greatest benefits of incorporating good relationship building skills into interactions with those you are helping is that, over time, they can become part of your "standard operating procedure" in your interaction with others. You will find many opportunities for communicating care in your relationships with family and friends—even strangers—at times when they need to talk about their concerns. At these times, knowing how to center, listen, and put your own concerns aside can keep the connections between you and others strong, healthy, and helpful.

The skills of caring communication are useful in casual relationships as well as close ones. Because the other person is in our lives only briefly, we may think that we do not need to attend to the quality of our connection. Perhaps we don't; usually we can do what we need to do simply by being civil. When we do take a moment to communicate care, the day is better for both of us.

I overheard two consecutive encounters in a store. The line at the check-out counter was very long because the cashier was training a new clerk. Both of them were harried. The first conversation went like this:

Customer: I can't believe how long this is taking.
Cashier: I'm sorry you have had to wait. We are training a new

clerk.
Customer: Why do you have to do this at the busiest times of day?
Cashier: Sorry, but there isn't any other time to do it.
Customer: This is a real inconvenience for customers, you know. There's always a rush at noon, and you should expect that.
Cashier: You know, maybe you should, too. There are other times to shop.

The transaction was completed in silence and took quite a bit of time because the senior cashier was angry and the new clerk was so flustered she kept making mistakes on the register. I could imagine the little black cloud a cartoonist might have drawn over the heads of this customer, the cashier, and the new clerk—and perhaps the rest of us who witnessed the encounter. The customer took her cloud with her, and everyone could feel the tension she had created.

The second conversation was quite different.

Customer: Boy, what a busy day.
Cashier: I'm sorry you have had to wait. We are training a new clerk.
Customer: (to new clerk): It seems to me that those computer registers are complicated. I'll bet it's a challenge for you to learn how to do this at the busiest time of day. [self-disclosure]
New clerk: It is, but it's the only time we have, and tomorrow I'll have to do this one my own.
Customer: All by yourself, huh? [reflection]
New clerk: Yes, I hope it won't be this busy.
Customer: It would be nice to have the first day on your own be a little more relaxed than this. [reflection]
New clerk: It sure would.

The transaction still took a long time because of the new clerk's unfamiliarity with the register. At the end, the customer thanked her, called her by name, and left, saying, *"It seems to me you're getting it, Peggy. Hang on in there. Good luck tomorrow!"* The new clerk looked relieved, and the senior cashier gave the customer a look of gratitude. All three of them smiled. The tension caused by the encounter between the employees and the first customer was gone.

This customer acted in a caring manner. The people involved in the conversation—and those of us around her—were affected in a positive way simply because she took time to acknowledge the cashier, care about the new clerk, and express understanding of the situation. Her interaction skills enhanced the quality of a brief encounter in a difficult situation. It was so much better not to have all that tension and frustration in addition to the long line!

The Heart of the Matter

If communicating care can make such a difference in a casual encounter, think of how much more it will make in a relationship characterized by love.

In a busy life, we may take our close relationships for granted and forget to take the time to attend to the quality of those relationships. We may not listen well, and we may respond in unhelpful ways. Our lack of attention to the relationship between us can strain or erode the sense of connection we have with the other person. As with helping relationships, the key influence on the quality of our lives together is the quality of the relationship we have, because the relationship is the only way we can know the other person and he can know us. We experience a high quality relationship as love.

When we experience unsteadiness in our love for another person or his love for us, it can be because we have not attended to the relationship between us with empathy, genuineness, and positive regard. We have some choices to make. We can choose to recommit to the relationship and invest healthy time and attention in it; we can let the relationship go because we no longer can give it what it needs to thrive; or we can find a way to renegotiate the relationship so that it better supports us and the other person. Any one of these courses of action is best accomplished with good helping communication skills.

It does take two people or more people to have a relationship. As a helper with good communication skills, we may be the one who has to take the first step in communicating care. It can be frustrating to be the one with the relationship building skills, but if we use our skills with loving intent, we are likely to be surprised at the returns we get on our investment of care. When we extend empathy, genuineness and positive regard to others, we usually get it back. When this happens, we are better able to build supportive, healthy relationships with those who matter the most.

When we communicate care, we demonstrate that we value other people; our positive regard is evident throughout our helping interaction. We make a difference—perhaps in a very small way, perhaps in only a brief moment. The size or duration of our contribution is not important. The process of moving toward making a difference at all is what counts.

This book began with the idea that the quality of the helping relationship matters most in determining the effectiveness of all our work with others. I believe that our fundamental job in life is *being* with others—and that that work surpasses all else we are drawn to doing. The quality of our lives is based on the quality of our relationships—big or little, permanent or brief, casual or committed. When we live with empathy, positive regard, and genuineness and communicate our care, we invite others to join us the heart of what matters.

AT THE HEART OF THE MATTER

29293361R00084

Made in the USA
Charleston, SC
07 May 2014